THE CULTS OF THE MOTHER GODDESSES IN INDIA

THE CULTS OF THE MOTHER GODDESSES IN INDIA

SOME NOTES ON HOMERIC FOLK-LORE

WILLIAM CROOKE

GYAN

Published by

Gyan Publishing House
5, Ansari Road
Daryaganj, New Delhi-110002
Phone: 011-47034999, 9811692060
E-mail: books@gyanbooks.com

Distribution Network
gyanbooks.com
India, USA, Canada, UK, Australia

ISBN: 978-93-7447-358-0 (HB)

First Published, 1908

2nd Impression 2025

Printed at: Gyan Press, Delhi.

THE CULTS OF THE MOTHER GODDESSES IN INDIA
Author: WILLIAM CROOKE

THE CULTS OF THE MOTHER GODDESSES IN INDIA

THE CULTS OF THE MOTHER GODDESSES IN INDIA.

BY W. CROOKE.

(*Read at the Meeting of the British Association, Bournemouth*, 11*th September*, 1919.)

BEHIND many divine impersonations of the Minoan and early Hellenic theogonies appears the majestic figure of the Great Mother, who is generally benevolent. "Just as the mother," says Dr. Farnell, "frequently stands between the children and the father as the mild intercessor, so the goddess often becomes the mediator of mercy to whom the sinners turn as their intercessor with the offended god. Such was Isis for the Graeco-Roman world; such at times was Athena for the Athenians; such is the Virgin for Mediterranean Christendom." [1] But the range of the Mother cult extends beyond the Mediterranean area, in forms like those of Nina or Ishtar in Babylonia, Ashtoreth, sister of Ishtar, among the Western Semites, the great Hittite Goddess of Boghaz-Keui.[2] As regards the Western Aryans, mythographers seem generally to have reached the conclusion that goddesses of this class should not be regarded as aliens, borrowed from the pre-Aryan races in whose lands they settled, and that, as the cults of Mother Earth prevailed widely in Europe, deities like Dione, Demeter, Hera and Hestia may be accepted as old Hellenic

[1] *Greece and Babylon*, 82.

[2] Sir J. G. Frazer, *The Golden Bough*, 3rd ed. *Adonis, Attis, Osiris*, i. 128 *et seqq*.

goddesses.[1] "The nature-worship of the Hellenes was pre-eminently concerned with Mother-earth—with Ge-meter, and this divine power in its varied personal forms was perhaps of all others the nearest and dearest to the popular heart: so much of their ritual was concerned directly with her. And some scholars have supposed, erroneously, I think, but not unnaturally, that all the leading Hellenic goddesses arose from this aboriginal animistic idea." [2]

At present our knowledge of these primitive Mother deities is far from being complete. As their cults and that of Mother Earth are widespread in India, it may be worth considering whether a description of them may throw some much-needed light on the origin and development of the Western Mothers.

The question of the transmission of culture is still a subject of active controversy, and I shall not attempt to decide whether India and the Mediterranean are in any true sense contiguous cultures. It may be admitted that the quest of the precious metals or minerals, incense, pepper and many other things may have led to early trade intercourse by the Red Sea route. But I do not think that any scholar, in the present state of our knowledge, would be inclined to trace much connexion in theology or ritual between India and Egypt. The case of the relations of India to Babylonia, the latter country forming a link with the West, is still obscure. There appears to be no Indian deity who can be compared with the Babylonian En-lil or Bel of Nippur, conceived as the god of earth *par excellence*; Mesopotamian religion has no parallel figure to the Grecian Ge, and though Ishtar possessed vegetative

[1] Farnell, *op. cit.* 94 *et seq.*

[2] *Ibid.* 114; *Id. Cults of the Greek States*, iii. 1 *et seqq.*, and compare Miss J. E. Harrison, *Journal Hellenic Society*, xix. (1899), 205, 208, 220 *et seq.*; *Prolegomena to the Study of Greek Religion*, 263 *et seqq.*; *Themis*, 166 *et seqq.*; *Mythology and Monuments of Ancient Athens*, 44.

functions, it would be hazardous to say that she was a personal form of Earth.[1]

The study of the Indian Mother cults is for many reasons ifficult. In their earliest forms they are aniconic and unco-ordinated, and literary evidence of the more primitive Dravidian cults is, of course, wanting. When they have been taken over by the Brāhmans they have been so worked over and metamorphosed that many of their original features are now unintelligible. When these deities influence fertility the cultus is to a large extent magical, and as magic necessarily involves secrecy, enquirers of a different faith are unable to investigate it. In the case of Saktism, the latest development, these difficulties are increased, because the worship of the female productive energies offends the nobler and more sober instincts of Hindus, and the rites are necessarily conducted with precautions against the intrusion of outsiders in the mysteries.

When we compare the Aryan and Dravidian pantheons in India an important difference at once attracts attention.[2] In Vedic belief and ritual goddesses occupy a very subordinate position, they play hardly any part as rulers of the world, and only two—Ushas, the spirit of the dawn, and Sarasvatī, originally the impersonation of a sacred river—acquired special importance.[3] In the same way, in Babylonia, except Ishtar, the goddesses are not very imposing figures, their characteristics are not sharply defined or differentiated, and their position conforms to the low conception of women in that civilisation.[4] In the modern

[1] M. Jastrow, *The Religion of Babylonia and Assyria*, 140; L. W. King, *Babylonian Religion and Mythology*, 10, 17; L. R. Farnell, *Greece and Babylon*, 114. On Babylonian influence in India, see A. A. Macdonell, A. B. Keith, *Vedic India*, i. 430 *et seq.*, ii. 128 *et seq.* 432.

[2] The distinctive difference between the Aryans and the Dasyu was one of religion—Macdonell-Keith, *Vedic Index*, i. 347, 357.

[3] A. A. Macdonell, *Vedic Mythology*, 124 *et seq.*; Sir R. G. Bhandarkar, *Vaisnavism, Saivism, and Minor Religious Systems*, 142 *et seqq.*

[4] L. W. King, *op. cit.* 22 *et seq.*

orthodox Brahmanical pantheon the male deities are also predominant, and their consorts, except in the cases of figures like Kālī, Durgā, or Devī, are of secondary importance. But in the old Dravidian pantheon which has survived in Southern India the leading feature is the worship of the female principle in nature, and it is only in the Brahman-ridden Tamil country that male deities acquire prominence over the goddesses.[1] The important, fundamental conception of Dyaus, the Sky-god, and Prithivi, "the broad one," the impersonation of the widespread northern plains, does appear in the Vedas, but this bears little relation to the worship of Mother Earth among the Indo-Aryan and Dravidian peoples.[2] In the Vedas "the Earth herself makes no remarkable figure: she is indeed deified, at least partially, is addressed as mother and substance of all things: is generally, in company with the sky, invoked to grant blessings; yet this never advanced further than a lively personation might go."[3]

In the later Hindu cults, however, that of Mother Earth has acquired great importance. She now takes the name, not of Prithivi, εὐρύστερνος of the Greeks, but of Bhūmi, "that which is produced, exists," or more generally of Dhartī, Dharanī, Dharitrī, "she who bears or carries," the upholder of the human, animal and vegetable creation which rests upon her surface. As a Grāmadevatā or village goddess she is generally aniconic, being supposed to dwell in a pile of rough stones or potsherds collected under

[1] Bishop H. Whitehead, *The Village Gods of South India*, 17, 94.

[2] Macdonell, *op. cit.* 8, 12; [Sir] E. B. Tylor, *Primitive Culture*, 2nd ed. i. 321 *et seqq.*; G. Oppert, *The Original Inhabitants of Bharatavarsa or India*, 402; A. A. Macdonell, A. B. Keith, *Vedic Index*, ii. 16 *et seq.*

[3] W. D. Whitney, *Oriental and Linguistic Studies*, 32. "The early Iranians personified Mother Earth as Spenta-Armaiti, the Aramati of the Vedas" (M. Haug, *Essays on the Sacred Language, Writings, and Religion of the Parsis*, 160, 274, 306; M. Geiger, *Civilization of the Eastern Iranians in Ancient Times*, i. *Introd.* xxxvii. *et seq.* 128 *et seq.*; A. A. Macdonell, *Vedic Mythology*, 119 *et seq.*)

the sacred tree of the community. Her cultus is of primitive simplicity: she is chiefly worshipped by women, and if she has a priest he is usually not a Brāhman, but drawn from the menials or outcastes. In south India Brāhmans object to serve the Mothers because they cannot join in their animal sacrifices.[1] In northern India her offerings consist usually of grain or fruit laid on her stones or of milk poured over them. The Orāon farmer, before transplanting his rice seedlings, makes a libation of rice-beer on the ground, and prays to Dhartī Māī: "O Mother Earth! May we have plenty of rain and a bumper crop! Here is a drink-offering for thee!"[2] The forest-dwelling Kharwār in Mirzapur, who now lives chiefly by farming, prays: "O Mother Earth! Keep in prosperity and protect the ploughman and his oxen!" while in the Panjāb the prayer runs: "Keep our rulers and bankers contented! Grant us a plentiful yield! So shall we pay our revenue and satisfy our banker"—the sinister figure who haunts the dreams of the struggling peasant.[3]

In the Vedas she is invoked to shelter the corpse as it is laid in the grave. "Go thou now to Mother Earth, who is wide-opened, favourable, a wool-soft maiden to the good man. May she guard thee from the lap of destruction! Be not oppressive to him, let him enter easily, may he fasten close to thee!"; or, as it runs in the Atharva-veda, "Be pleasant to him, O Earth, a thornless resting-place: furnish him with a broad refuge! I cover thee excellently with the garment of Mother Earth! Thou being earth, I make thee enter into earth!"[4] The Rāūls of Poona at the present day, who bury their dead, say: "O Mother Earth! we make this body over to thee in the presence of the gods Brahmā and Vishnu, who are our witnesses."

[1] Bishop H. Whitehead, *op. cit.* 41.

[2] Sarat Chandra Roy, *The Orāons of Chota Nāgpur*, 142.

[3] W. Crooke, *Popular Religion and Folklore of Northern India*, i. 32 *et seq.*

[4] *Rig-Veda*, x. 18: *Atharvaveda*, xviii. 2, 4, trans. W. D. Whitney, ii. 836, 843, 883. The word for "earth" is here *bhūmi*.

Here the primitive animistic belief has been worked over by Brahmanism.

So far we have been considering the cultus in its most primitive type: but the oriental tendency towards anthropomorphism rapidly begins to affect it, and the representation of the goddess develops into the iconic stage. The southern Mother, Ellammā, is depicted rising from the earth as in the Buddhist sculptures the Earth Goddess emerges from the earth to support the horse on which Gautama rides, when he leaves his wife and home and makes the Great Renunciation, and in Greek art the Anadosis or up-rising of the Earth Goddess, Pandora, is a favourite subject.[1] As regards the cultus, the advance towards anthropomorphism is marked by the belief current in Bengal that at the first burst of the rains in June-July, Mother Earth, in order to prepare herself for her fertilizing work, is supposed to menstruate. During this time there is an entire cessation from all ploughing, sowing, and other farm work; widows abstain from eating rice; next comes the rite of purification, when a stone representing the goddess is fixed erect in the ground, its top is smeared with vermilion, a survival of a blood sacrifice, the housewife bathes it with turmeric water, a betelnut is placed on a piece of wood close by, the stone is bedecked with flowers, and offerings of milk and flowers are made.[2] A similar rite of purification, under Brāhman auspices, is performed in the case of the goddess Bhāgavatī, "the Venerable, Divine One," at her temple in Travancore, after her menstruation, which is supposed to take place eight or ten times during the year.[3]

[1] B. Ziegenbalg, *Genealogy of the South Indian Gods*, 137; A. Grünwedel, *Buddhist Art in India*, 98 *et seqq.*; Miss J. E. Harrison, *Prolegomena to the Study of Greek Religion*, 276 *et seqq.*; *Id. Mythology and Monuments of Ancient Athens*, *Introd.* xxix. *et seq.*, li. 449; L. R. Farnell, *Cults of the Greek States*, iii. 17, 25, 27, 55, 216.

[2] [Sir] E. Gait, *Census Report*, *Bengal*, 1901, i. 189.

[3] V. Nagam Aiya, *Travancore State Manual*, ii. 89 *et seq.*

Again, the Earth Goddess, being the primary source of that Mana which fertilizes men and animals, and brings the fruits of the earth to harvest, naturally becomes periodically exhausted, and needs repose to recruit her energies. In Malabar in January-February the field work is over, and Mother Earth rests during the hot weather until the first shower of rain, when she revives and undergoes the natural function of women just described.[1] This periodical rest of the goddess, to which further reference will be made later on, is observed throughout the country in various ways. In the Panjāb she sleeps on seven or eight days in each month, and on these days ploughing and sowing are tabu, with this concession that if inadvertently work has started on these days, it may be finished.[2] In the Deccan, after the Naurātrī, or Nine Nights' feast of the goddess in September-October, her temple is closed from the sacred 11th day of the month until the full-moon day, while the goddess rests and refreshes herself after the liberal distribution of Mana to her worshippers during her festival.[3] In the Deccan many people make a vow to live during the rest of the goddess in the country north of the river Godāvarī, this being regarded as the southern boundary, marking off Hindostan from the non-Aryan tribes of the south.[4]

Naturally after her periodical rest the Earth Mother needs to be aroused. This rite goes back to Vedic times, when, at the Mahāvrata festival, maidens carrying water pitchers used to dance round a fire and sing: "The cows smell pleasantly: here is sweet drink! the cows are

[1] L. K. Anantha Krishna Iyer, *The Cochin Tribes and Castes*, ii. 78.

[2] *North Indian Notes and Queries*, ii. 172; *Panjāb Notes and Queries*, ii. 205.

[3] *Bombay Gazetteer*, xx. 444.

[4] M. M. Underhill, *The Indian Year*, 14. "The Phrygians, according to Plutarch, believed that their god slept in winter and waked in summer, and accordingly they celebrated with Bacchic rites the beginning and end of this period of rest" (Sir J. G. Frazer, *The Golden Bough*, 3rd ed. *Adonis, Attis, Osiris*, ii. 41).

mothers of butter: sweet drink! the cows we here bathe: sweet drink!" As they danced they struck their right thighs with their right hands—probably with the intention of expelling evil influences and promoting fertility: or they used to beat the earth with their right feet, and danced, following the course of the sun.[1] At the sowing rite of the Garos the priest invokes Rokimē, "Mother of rice," and striking the earth with a chopper-handle reminds the goddess that certain flowers have blossomed in the jungle, which is a sign that it is now time to sow the rice of which she is the Mother.[2] With this beating of the ground with a chopper-handle we may compare the Greek vase painting interpreted by Miss J. E. Harrison, where a Satyr is beating the ground to wake the Earth Mother, Pandora.[3] At the Orāon Jeth Jātra festival, according to Colonel Dalton,[4] the girls used to pat the Earth to make her fruitful. Later enquiries, however, show that it is the young men who carry fans made of wild date leaves, or yak tails, which they wave over the Earth as if coaxing her to bear abundant crops. Mr. Sarat Chandra Roy points out that, in Orāon belief, this is the function of males, not of women. Hence women are not allowed to plough or sow, but they may transplant the rice seedlings after they have been grown by the men, because it is the business of women to tend them, as they do in the case of their own babies.[5] The first act done when a male child is born among the Nāyars of Malabar is to beat the Earth with a coconut leaf, or, in the case of a girl, to grind some turmeric in a mortar. This

[1] A. B. Keith, "The Vedic Mahāvrata," *Transactions Third International Congress for the History of Religion*, ii. 55.

[2] A. Playfair, *The Garos*, 93.

[3] *Journal Hellenic Society*, xx. (1900), 106 *et seq.*, xxi. (1901), 6; L. R. Farnell, *Cults of the Greek States*, iii. 26, 112, 205.

[4] *Descriptive Ethnology of Bengal*, 198.

[5] Sarat Chandra Roy, *op. cit.* 320. For a doubtful example of thrashing the Earth to make her fruitful from New Caledonia, see E. S. Hartland, *Primitive Paternity*, i. 111 note.

is done, it is said, with the object of removing the child's fear, and part of the puberty rites of the Paraiyans is for the mother to strike the ground behind her son with a rice-pestle.[1] The meaning of these rites is obscure: possibly they may be fertility observances intended to arouse the Earth Mother to strengthen the boy.

The great gods, Vishnu and others, also sleep from June-July till October-November, that is to say, during the rainy season when field work is slack. The same considerations, based on the cessation of work during the rains, account for the annual Buddhist Retreat (varsika, vassa, vassavasa), during which the monks ceased to make their usual visits to their disciples.[2] The similar Retreat of the Jains (pajjusana, pachusan) should be held when the rainy season is well advanced, a time when ordinary work is interrupted, and there is danger of destruction of life, animal and vegetable, which is then abundant.[3]

Similar animistic beliefs regarding the personification of Mother Earth and the danger of destroying the life which she fosters account for the prejudice against agriculture which prevails among some tribes, castes, or religious orders. The Laws of Manu, the official manual of Brahmanical social observances, direct that a Brāhman or a Kshatriya shall carefully avoid agriculture, "which causes injury to many beings and depends on others. Some declare that agriculture is something excellent, but that means of subsistence is blamed by the virtuous: for the wooden implement with iron point injures the Earth and the beings living in the Earth."[4] A religious sanction was thus given to the prejudice against agriculture, work which

[1] E. Thurston, *Castes and Tribes of Southern India*, v. 344, vi. 93.

[2] H. Kern, *Manual of Indian Buddhism*, 80 *et seq.*; C. J. F. S. Forbes, *British Burma and its People*, 170; Shway Yoe, *The Burman*, i. 263; L. A. Waddell, *The Buddhism of Thibet*, 223 *et seq.*

[3] Mrs. M. Stevenson, Hastings: *Encyclopaedia of Religion and Ethics*, v. 675.

[4] Manu, *Laws*, x. 84, 85; cf. Sir J. G. Frazer, *Golden Bough*, 3rd ed. *Adonis, Attis, Osiris*, i. 88 *et seqq.*

was not suited to the Aryan priest and warrior. Hence they were in the habit of making it over to the autochthonous peoples, and many Rājputs and Brāhmans at the present day will not handle the plough. Buddhists adopted the same rule on account of the danger likely to be caused to animal or vegetable life by ploughing: but they were forced to make an ingenious compromise, to wit, that a man should not till land for his own advantage, but that to do so for the benefit of the Buddhist Sanga, or community, was not opposed to the teaching of the master.[1] In the same way, the Jains are particularly careful not to destroy all animal and some vegetable life. They object to build a house, to till a field, to eat earth-grown vegetables, like potatoes, beet, or onions, but they will eat oranges or mangoes, which, being in the air, do not form a refuge for life (jiva): a pious member of the sect must never sell artificial manure, as it is sometimes made from the bones of dead animals, or take a contract for building houses or digging wells, because an insect may be destroyed in the course of the work: for the same reason the trade of a blacksmith is tabu among them.[2] Hence also arose the custom of having the first ploughing done by one of the menial tribes, like the Kurumbas of southern India, who risked the danger which his masters were afraid to face.[3] The King, being sacrosanct, was also required to do the sacred ploughing.[4]

[1] I-tsing, *A Record of the Buddhist Religion as practised in India and the Malay Archipelago*, trans. J. Takakusu, 61.

[2] Mrs. M. Stevenson, *The Heart of Jainism*, 115, 138, 141, 214, 223. "The Bhātias, traders in Cutch, will not deal in vegetables or root crops" (*Bombay Gazetteer*, v. 54).

[3] Thurston, *op. cit.* iv. 168; F. Metz, *The Tribes inhabiting the Neilgherry Hills*, 116; *Folk-Lore*, iv. 215.

[4] Sir J. Bowring, *The Kingdom and People of Siam*, i. 158; H. C. Warren, *Buddhism in Translations*, 54; *The Jātaka*, Cambridge trans. iv. 104; [Sir] J. G. Scott, J P. Hardiman, *Gazetteer of Upper Burma and the Shan States*, part 1, vol. i. 52, vol. ii. 101; Sir J. G. Frazer, *Pausanias*, ii. 172, 489, 514; *The Golden Bough*, 3rd ed. *The Dying God*, 149 *et seq.*

It is needless to discuss the many beliefs implying that Mother Earth in India is regarded as the prime source of Mana. One rite, specially connected with fertility, deserves notice. All over the country, as part of the marriage ceremony, the women of the family go to the village clay-pit, and bring from thence the Matmangarā, or "lucky earth," which is generally used in building the fireplace on which the materials of the wedding feast are cooked.[1] In southern India this "lucky earth" is brought from an anthill, because ants which swarm in numbers are a type of fertility.[2] Other circumstances enhance the luck of such earth. In Poona seven kinds of "lucky earth" are brought—from a Kings' palace gate, from a hill, from under the foot of an elephant or of a horse, from a place where four roads meet, from a cowshed, and from under the sacred *vāla* tree (*andropogon muricatum*).[3] At a Rājput wedding in Bījāpur, a relative of the bridegroom goes to the bank of a river or a tank and worships Mother-Earth by pouring water on her surface: he daubs the place with sandalwood paste, and throws rice and flowers on it: then he loosens a clod with a pickaxe and brings it to the marriage booth.[4] In the Telugu country, the earth, known as "Golden produce," is brought from a tank with much ceremony by five women—a lucky number—who are accompanied by a band of music, and they have a cloth held over them as a canopy, probably to protect them from the Evil Eye and from the attacks of malignant spirits; it is added to a pile of earth, decorated with coloured pigments, which is raised in the marriage shed, and beside it the bride and bridegroom sit; the pile is not removed, but left untouched until wind and rain destroy it.[5] At a

[1] W. Crooke, *op. cit.* i. 27.

[2] Thurston, *op. cit.* vi. 355. "The anthill, being sacred, is often used as a shrine of the village goddess" (Bishop Whitehead, *op. cit.* 79).

[3] *Bombay Gazetteer*, xviii. part I, 141 note.

[4] *Ibid.* xxiii. 159.

[5] J. A. Padfield, *The Hindu at Home*, 144.

Brāhman wedding in Gujarāt, the earth is used for making the altars used in the rite known as Grihasānti, or "planet-soothing," by which the dangerous influence of some planet, which would mar the success of the marriage, is removed.[1] The intention of these ceremonies is probably to convey to the married pair the fertilizing Mana of Mother Earth.

When Mother Earth is thus regarded by the Hindus as a living creature they unconsciously confirm the latest conclusions of science. The well-known French agronomist, M. G. Dumont, has recently shown that the Earth is a living organism, and that the earthy elements are merely the skeleton which holds together its respiratory, digestive and muscular portions. Respiration is the interchange of gases, the digestive apparatus the interspaces supplying nutritive liquids to the plant roots, the muscular action the contractions which excite coagulation, and which are due to the colloidal membranes covering the earth particles. Folklore, as is often the case, is thus justified by the conclusions of science.

Thus far we have been considering Mother Earth in her benign, kindly aspects, as the maintainer and giver of fertility to men, animals, and plants, the patron goddess of agriculture, in which respects she is the counterpart of the Hellenic and other deities of the West. In this aspect she is closely connected with the cult of trees, which force their roots into her bosom, and draw support from her, while by their branches they link her with the spirits of the air. So in Greece, Europa, "the broad-faced," the equivalent of the Hindu Prithivi, probably a Cretan-Boeotian form of the Earth Goddess, was worshipped at Gortyna in a sacred tree.[2] In India, as we have seen, she is associated with the communal tree, the planting of which is the first act in the foundation of a new village. But, at the same time, the tree acts as a prophylactic, because it

[1] *Bombay Gazetteer*, ix. part 1, 42 *et seq.*

[2] A. B. Cook, *Zeus*, i. 537; Farnell, *op. cit.* iii. 14, 30.

gives shelter to all sorts of malevolent spirits which beset the inhabitants. A curious instance of this belief comes from Poona. When his parents murdered the Marātha Peshwa, Nārāyanrāv in 1772, his successor, after two intervening members of the house, Bājīrāv, who believed himself to be haunted by Nārāyanrāv's ghost, planted several hundred thousand mango trees round the city to afford a shelter to the angry spirit.[1] In connexion with the fertility cult, the value of the tree is improved if it be ceremonially wedded to another tree.

Near every village of the Pāvrās, a forest tribe in Khāndesh, is a sacred tree, round which, before harvest, the villagers prostrate themselves before the rising Sun, offer grain, and sacrifice goats and flowers. This tree god, known as Bāvā, or "Father," Kumbā, has a consort, Rānī, "Queen," Kājhal, who lives in another sacred tree not far off.[2] Hence, the Mother Goddess, like Sijū, the Kāchāri god, often lives in a tree. The Rājput legend tells that their patron goddess Āsāpūrnā, "Fulfiller of desires," appeared out of a tree to protect the princess Surabhī, when, a fugitive, she lay almost at the point of death under its shade.[3]

Particularly among races who bury their dead, the Earth Mother is apt to assume a chthonic and malignant character. In India, as in Greece,[4] the snake forms the link between the benign spirits, ancestral or other, and the malevolent earth genii. In Bundelkhand certain snakes known as Bhiarānī, a word interpreted to mean, "Dwellers in the Earth," are regarded as forms of Devī, the Mother Goddess: coconuts are offered to them by priests drawn from the menial castes, while a Brāhman generally lives close by and receives a share of the offerings.[5] In the

[1] *Bombay Gazetteer*, xviii. part 1, 293.

[2] *Ibid.* xii. 97.

[3] Playfair, *op. cit.* 18; J. Tod, *Annals of Rajasthan*, ed. 1919, iii. 1461.

[4] Miss J. E. Harrison, *Journal Hellenic Society*, xix. (1899), 213.

[5] C. E. Luard, *Census Report, Central India*, 1901, i. 75.

Chambā State, on the borders of Kashmīr, the Devīs are goddesses who have power to cure diseases in man and beast; they are not, like the Nāgs, or true serpent deities, associated with springs, but it is common to find Nāg and Devī temples side by side, and similar attributes are assigned to both.[1] On the other hand, these Devīs, as promoters of fertility, are worshipped in Bashahr in the forms of little girls.[2]

This chthonic aspect of the Mother Goddess may be illustrated by the custom of burying in the earth portions of the victims dedicated to her. When a careful Athenian went to gather a certain medicinal root, he used to place in the hole a honeyed cake as an offering to Gaia, the Earth Mother.[3] For the same reason, at the Thesmophoria festival, live pigs were thrown into the underground sanctuaries of the goddess.[4] The pig, possibly on account of its habit of rooting up the ground to obtain food, was the sacred animal of Demeter and Kore.[5] In southern India, at the worship of the Grāmadevatā, or village goddess, a buffalo, which is also possibly on account of its black colour and brutish appearance a chthonic animal, the beast upon which Yama, god of death, rides, is buried in a pit close to the boundary stone which is occupied by the goddess.[6] In the same part of the country we find the custom of burying a live pig in the village street, where the cattle pass in and out on their way from and to the fields, probably as a prophylactic propitiation of the Earth Mother: in some cases the pig is buried up to the neck

[1] H. A. Rose, *Glossary of the Tribes and Castes of the Punjab and the North-Western Frontier Province*, i. 331.

[2] *Ibid.* i. 479.

[3] Farnell, *op. cit.* iii. 15. [4] *Ibid.* iii. 89 *et seqq.*

[5] Miss J. E. Harrison, *Prolegomena to the Study of Greek Religion*, 122; J. C. Lawson, *Modern Greek Folklore and Ancient Greek Religion*, 87; Sir J. Frazer, *The Golden Bough*, 3rd ed. *Spirits of the Corn and the Wild*, ii. 16 *et seqq.*

[6] Bishop H. Whitehead, *op. cit.* 108, 111, 113.

at the entrance of the village, and the cattle are driven over it until it is trampled to death, while rice stained with the blood of a sacrificed lamb is scattered over the herd.[1] The Goālas, herdsmen in northern India, turn a pig loose amidst a herd of buffalos, which are encouraged to gore it to death.[2]

It has been assumed by some scholars, as has already been stated, that the cults of the Mother goddesses, benevolent or malignant, have all been derived from that of Mother Earth, in these differing, but complementary manifestations. This theory has been disputed by orthodox Brāhman writers, like Pandit Harikishan Kaul.[3] He, by a method characteristic of Hindus discussing their own religion, traces all these goddess cults back to the Vedas, maintaining that there is but one original Mother Goddess, that the later forms are developments of her worship, and denying that these have any connexion with Mother Earth. "The personification of the powers of the Creator, the Preserver, and the Destroyer being once established, the identification of any one of them with important, uncommon, or uncontrollable phenomena is an easy matter." But we have already seen that in the Vedas the goddesses hold a subordinate position, and this theory ignores the distinctively local character of the worship. It is not from any original Vedic goddess that the modern worshipper of great personalities, like Tuljā Bhavānī in the Nizam's Dominion, Ambā Bhavānī of Mount Abu in Rajputana, Hinglāj Mātā in Balochistan, or the mighty Kālī of Calcutta, traces his devotion. The process by which these great personalities acquired their present reputation was clearly because, for some reason, the local cult from which they were derived gained the credit of wonder-working beyond the small

[1] Bishop H. Whitehead, *op. cit.* 52, 58, 59.

[2] [Sir] H. Risley, *Tribes and Castes of Bengal*, i. 290; *Folk-Lore*, xxviii. 154 *et seqq.*

[3] *Census Report*, *Panjab*, 1911, i. 114 *et seqq.*

circle of their original worshippers. In other words, the conception of a single great goddess,—Devī, Durgā, Kālī,—is later in order of time than the local cult out of which it originated.

The facts already stated lead to the inevitable conclusion that many of the Mother goddesses have been developed from the Grāmadevatā, or village goddesses, many of whom owe their origin to the cult of Mother Earth. The benignant and chthonic, or malignant, manifestations of this Earth goddess account for the two distinct types which we find among the Mothers as a class. The localisation of function in the case of the village goddesses opens the way for the specialisation of the Mothers, many of whom ultimately come to be regarded as responsible for distinct spheres of activity; various classes of disease, for instance, being made over to distinct deities. But this is a later development, the Mothers, as well as the other deities of Hinduism, being in their most primitive types deities "of all work." This does not affect the theological so much as the practical aspect—the cultus. "The really important question," as Robertson Smith puts it, "is not what a god has power to do, but whether I can get him to do it for me, and this depends upon the relation in which he stands to me." [1]

At the same time, in dealing with a complex polytheism like that of Hinduism, it is rash to assume a single origin for a group of deities, with infinitely varied legends of origin and cult ritual. And there are types which cannot readily be derived from the Earth Mother.

In the first place, we have the group of the Forest Mothers. While the village Mothers, as representing the agricultural stage, may be propitiated with animal sacrifice, there is no evidence that the dweller in the jungle offers the produce of the chase, a boar or a stag, to his Mother goddess. The common method of propitiating them is for each passer-by

[1] *The Religion of the Semites*, 2nd ed. 83.

to add a stick or a stone to the rude heap which marks the abiding-place of the deity. In the Vedas large trees, called Vanaspati, are addressed as deities, and the forest, as a whole, appears as a goddess under the name of Aranyānī, called "Mother of beasts," abounding in food without tillage, in whose dark solitudes various uncanny sounds are weirdly described.[1] Aranyānī has now passed out of popular knowledge, but Vanaspati, in the form of Bansaptī Mā, "Mistress of the wood," is, in Northern India, propitiated by flinging a stone or branch on her cairn, either as a mode of keeping the spirit under control,[2] or as a tribute to, or recognition of, the dreaded deity who abides in the dark places of the jungle. But she is developing into a goddess of the agricultural type, because village herdsmen who graze their herds in the jungle offer to her a cock, a goat, or a young pig, with a prayer that she will protect the cattle from tigers.[3] In the Central Provinces the cult of Banjārī Deo, possibly a deified member of the Banjārā carrier tribe who used to drive their cattle along the jungle paths, is so imperfectly organised that the deity who dwells in a cairn to which every one adds a stone, may be male or female.[4] The Paniyans, a forest tribe in Madras, worship a female, Kad Bhāgavatī, or a sexless deity called Kulī, who dwells in a stone or cairn.[5] Major Tremearne[6] suggests, in the case of Hausa deities, that this uncertainty about sex may depend upon a change from polyandry to polygamy, or upon the relations of the goddess with her consort; but this does not seem to apply to Indian deities of this class, who are so vaguely conceived that the question of sex becomes immaterial. Goddesses

[1] A. A. Macdonell, *Vedic Mythology*, 154. "Vanaspati, 'Lord of the forest,' in the Vedas primarily denotes tree" (*Id.* and A. B. Keith, *Vedic Index*, ii. 241).

[2] Sir J. G. Frazer, *The Golden Bough*, 3rd ed. *The Scapegoat*, 15 *et seqq*.

[3] Crooke, *op. cit.* i. 115.

[4] A. E. Nelson, *Gazetteer of Bilāspur District*, i. 74.

[5] Thurston, *op. cit.* vi. 62.

[6] *The Ban of the Bori*, 418.

of this type do not appear to be connected with the cult of Mother Earth because their worshippers are in the pre-agricultural stage.

Secondly, there is a type of Mothers who are generally acknowledged to be of human origin. Many of the southern Mothers fall into this category, such as Gangammā, sometime regarded as a form of the divine river Ganges, who is also said to have been the daughter of a Brāhman, and Pangammā, one of three sisters who made a famous tank.[1] This type of Mother is particularly common in Gujarāt in the shape of the deified spirits of women of the Chāran tribe, people who, in the old days of anarchy, used to take charge of convoys of treasure, and were ready to give their lives in its defence. The murderer of such guardians was believed to be haunted by the angry spirits of his victims, and even now, though their traditional occupation has ceased, Chāran women are supposed to possess supernatural powers, and are addressed as "Mother," or "Goddess Mother." Many of the most famous Mother Goddesses in Gujarāt belong to this class.[2]

Thirdly, we must not dismiss the possibility that some Mothers may be simply animistic or pre-animistic spirits, impersonation of the awe and terror with which people of the lower culture regard anything quaint or abnormal. Possibly some of the Jungle Mothers may be included in this class.

But the general class of Mothers is so vague, "figures as melting and shifting as the clouds of sunset"—so Andrew Lang described the Vedic gods[3]—that the study of their origin and relations is difficult. In their earliest forms they are purely local, regarded as having no relation to the

[1] A. F. Cox, A. H. Stuart, *Manual of the North Arcot District*, i. 186. See other instances in Bishop Whitehead, *op. cit.* 26, 32, 75, 118, 123.

[2] A. K. Forbes, *Rās Māla*, 2nd ed. 426 ff; *Bombay Gazetteer*, v. 76, vii. 609 *et seqq.*, ix. part 1, *Introd.* xxxvi; Sir M. Monier-Williams, *Brahmanism and Hinduism*, 4th ed. 225 *et seq.*

[3] *Myth, Ritual, and Religion*, i. 161.

world as a whole. But when they are adopted by Hinduism they become great deities whose sphere of action is unlimited. These two conceptions, as well as their kindly and malevolent manifestations everywhere intermingle, and cannot readily be distinguished. As Bishop Whitehead remarks, to the peasant of South India they are neither exclusively evil spirits nor unmixed benefactors: they are of uncertain temper and very human in their liability to take offence.[1] It might have been expected that much help would be derived from their cult titles, a study of which has been so fruitful in explaining the Hellenic pantheon. But the most common epithets are vague—Mātā or Mā, "Mother," Devī, "The Divine One," or, vaguer still they are known as Grāmadevatā, "Village Godlings," or even in north India as Dih, "The Village." The same goddess may be, on her kindly side, Lakshmī or Srī, goddess of good fortune, now consort of Vishnu:[2] Lokamātā, "World Mother"; Āsāpūrnā, "Fulfiller of Desires"; Annapūrnā, καρποφόρος, "She that fills men with grain," or Sākambharī, "Nourisher of Herbs," the counterpart of Demeter Chloe, goddess of young corn and other vegetation. On the other side she may be Durgā in her varied forms, or Kālī, "The Black One," Demeter the Black, whom Mr. R. V. Russell calls a deified tigress. Some titles are purely euphemistical, based on the theory that by the use of a flattering divine name, the worshipper, if he has really learnt it, may coerce the deity to grant his desires.

Many names are pure inventions of the Brāhman officiants, many, and perhaps the most popular mark the local character of the cult.

[1] *Op. cit.* 25.

[2] "Her name appears as early as the *Satapatha Brāhmana* (A. A. Macdonell, A. B. Keith, *Vedic Index*). Rhys Davids, *Buddhist India*, 217 *et seq.* "She is represented in Buddhist sculptures seated on a lotus while two elephants pour water over her" (A. Grünwedel, *Buddhist Art in India*, 39).

We have seen that in the Vedas, as well as in Babylonia, the cult of goddesses is subordinate to that of gods. The Vedic Hindus were in the agricultural stage, but they had only recently emerged from the pastoral. And much of the work of tilling the soil was probably done by the aboriginal races whom the Aryans found in occupation.[1] This contempt for agriculture has descended to some modern Rājputs and Brāhmans. We have, therefore, to look for the origins of Mother worship to these indigenous people which we may call Dravidian, or Mon-khmer.

It seems dangerous to press too far in theory that the worship of the Mothers depends upon the leading part played by women in agriculture in many primitive societies, and among some of the present Indian tribes and castes.[2] Nor does it seem to be connected with Mother Right. In India, as is the case elsewhere, agricultural ceremonies and the culture of the local gods are often entrusted to women because they are more emotional, believed to be in closer touch with the spirit world, endowed with a stronger fertility Mana than that possessed by men. But the appointment of women as regular priestesses seems to be uncommon, Bishop Whitehead mentioning an exceptional case in the worship of the Mother goddess Nakulammā.[3] There does not appear to be any sound evidence that the cults of the Mothers in India were, to any special extent, dependent upon the cooperation of women in agriculture, a cooperation which, as we have seen in the case of a primitive tribe like the Orāons, is carefully restricted. It may be

[1] B. H. Baden-Powell, *The Indian Village Community*, 188. The facts are collected in a convenient shape by P. T. Srinivas Iyengar, *Life in Ancient India in the Age of the Mantras*, 23 *et seqq.* The views of Baden-Powell are criticised by Macdonell-Keith, *Vedic Index*, i. 182, ii. 173, 254, 333 *et seq.*, who describe the importance of agriculture in Vedic times.

[2] F. B. Jevons, *Introduction to the History of Religion*, 1st ed. 239 *et seqq.*; Miss J. E. Harrison, *Prolegomena to the Study of Greek Religion*, 272; and compare Professor Gilbert Murray, *Four Stages in Greek Religion*, 78.

[3] *Op. cit.* 63.

suggested that it was as agents of fertility in general that the Mothers were deified. These cults, in their more ecstatic or hysterical form, prevail chiefly among the Dravidians of the south, where they are connected with practices like devil-dancing, spirit possession and the like, which are less common among the more sober and less excitable races of northern India. In that part of the country it is only in places outside Āryāvarta, the original Holy Land in the south-western Panjab, that the more brutal forms of animal sacrifice and ecstatic rites are found, as at the shrine of Kālī in Calcutta, Kāmākhyā in Assam, Devī Pātan in northern Oudh, and in Nepāl.[1]

The explanation, again, of Bishop Whitehead,[2] that the cult was based on Totemism, does not seem to be convincing. So far as we are acquainted with the principles of Totemism in India it seems to have affected social institutions much more than religious beliefs or ritual.

When Mother worship is taken over by Brahmanism it exhibits those naive attempts at organisation and the otiose symbolism and ritual which are characteristic of that form of belief. The Mothers are usually classed in well-defined groups, sometimes of seven, eight, nine or sixteen.[3] Their powers and activities in special fields are more carefully discriminated. In the standard form of ritual current in the lower Himālaya they are worshipped in connexion with Ganesa, lord of luck and controller of enterprises, as a preface to the other rites. The celebrant takes a plank, cleanses it with rice flour, and on its surface draws seven figures representing the Mothers, with Ganesa on the right, and on the left a representation of the Moon. He then makes a brush out of five or six stalks of the sacred *dūb* (*cynodon dactylon*) grass, and dipping it in cowdung,

[1] W. Ward, *The Hindoos*, 2nd ed. ii. 115 *et seqq.*; *Gazetteer of Oudh*, 1877, i. 367 *et seqq.*; H. H. Oldfield, *Sketches from Nepal*, ii 293 *et seq.*

[2] *Op. cit.* 146 *et seqq.*

[3] Oppert, *op. cit.* 447 *et seqq.*; Ziegenbalg, *op. cit.* 36, 133.

anoints with it each of the Mothers, recites verses of praise in their honour, pours a libation of butter and sugar over the figures, waves a lamp before them, and offers flowers. The rite ends with the recital of a hymn in their honour, the celebrant receives his fee, and in return places a flower from the offering on the head of the person at whose expense the ceremony has been performed.[1] In another form of the ritual the Mothers are symbolised by a series of earthen pots in which they are supposed to dwell, reared in piles, and placed in the marriage shed as dispensers of fertility.[2] In southern India we meet a special Pot goddess, and at the Durgā Pūjā festival in Bengal the installation of the goddess in a pot is a prominent part of the rites.[3]

It is at present impossible to give even a summary sketch of the cultus of the Mothers. Much has been done in southern India by workers like Bishop Whitehead and Mr. F. J. Richards : but much further enquiry is necessary before this interesting phase of Indian popular religion is thoroughly explored. The personality of these deities is still imperfectly known. In many places the goddess is at once maid and mother, like Demeter and Kore, and year by year, as Hera did by bathing in the Canathus spring, she renews her virginity, only to lose it again when she performs a ritual marriage at the sowing or harvest festival.[4] In the case of Demeter and Kore it has been assumed that the former represents the true Earth goddess, her daughter being the impersonation of the young earth and vegetation in spring.[5] This is probably true in the case of the Hellenic goddesses, but it may be suggested that in India the personification of mother and virgin is based on the perio-

[1] Atkinson, *op. cit.* ii. 834 *et seq.* For a full account of the rites at the temple of the famous Baroda Mother goddess, Bechrājī, see *Bombay Gazetteer*, vii. 609 *et seqq.*

[2] See a photograph in Thurston, *op. cit.* vi. 19.

[3] Oppert, *op. cit.* 503 ; Pratapa Chandra Ghosha, *The Durga Puja*, 32 *et seqq.*

[4] Pausanias, ii. 38, 2.

[5] Farnell, *op. cit.* iii. 116.

dical renewal and loss of virginity after a ritual marriage. At any rate, the cult of the Virgins side by side with that of the Mothers is not uncommon. In southern India seven Virgins are worshipped, and in the Panjab some rugged rocks are called Kunwārī, or the Virgins, to commemorate, it is said, a party of maidens who were killed to save their honour, and deified after death.[1] We also meet, from the Vedic age down to modern times, the cult of pairs of twins, often brother and sister.[2]

As we have seen, the Mother, exhausted by her labours, needs periodical rest to renew her strength. The same result is also provided by two methods : the sacred marriage, the *ἱερὸς γάμος* of Greek ritual, and by blood sacrifice.

As regards the sacred marriage—we must be on our guard in accepting the numerous cases in which the Mother is regarded as the consort of some deity, unless we can actually prove a ritualistic marriage. The Brahmanical craze for uniformity usually leads them to class the divine pair as wife and her consort. Among the Dravidians, who are less exposed to Brāhman influence, we have many cases of the sacred marriage. The Malayālīs annually marry their god Sevarāyan to the goddess who is the presiding deity of the Kāvērī river.[3] Though there is no direct evidence of a ritual marriage, some goddesses are closely connected with a male, as in the case of Orasandiammā and Samalammā, tutelary goddesses of the Vāda fishermen, associated, the former with Rāmasondī, who is her brother, and the latter, curiously enough, with the image of a Bengali Babu on horseback.[4] In many parts of Madras, Poturāzū is at once husband, brother, and

[1] Bishop Whitehead, *op. cit.* 101 ; Rose, *op. cit.* i. 131.

[2] E. W. Hopkins, *The Religions of India*, 83 note. "Incest was recognised in Vedic times, as appears from the legend of the marriage of Yama and Yamī, brother and sister" (A. A. Macdonell, A. B. Keith, *Vedic Index*, i. 397).

[3] Thurston, *op. cit.* iv. 415 *et seqq.*

[4] *Ibid.* vii. 261 *et seq.*, 264.

attendant of the goddess Dayamavvā.[1] In Bengal, several gods and goddesses of the Tipārā tribe are married to each other; in the Rajshahī District the Sun is married to Chhatmātā, the Sixth Day Mother, so called because this is the date of her festival: Koilā Mātā, a Mother goddess of Bihār, is sometimes conceived to be a male, Koilā Bābā, and when a well is being excavated a male image of wood is made and married to that of the goddess: Hudum Deo, who is now beginning to be identified with the Vedic Indra, is worshipped by the Rājbansīs of Dinājpur in androgynous form—two figures made of clay or cowdung representing, the one a male, the other a female: Ghantā Karanā is consort of Sītala, the small-pox goddess.[2] The classical case from Bengal is the marriage by the Orāons of the Earth with the Sun, with formal rites, in spring when the Sāl tree blossoms.[3] In Chota Nāgpur we have one of the best instances in the case of the Kharwār goddess, Mūchak Rānī, which I have elsewhere published.[4] Among the Kandhs, Burā Pennū, god of light, has, as his consort, Tārā Pennū, the Earth goddess.[5] In Central India, Kamparavara, a god of the Bhīl tribe, is married to the goddess Kajal, and at the Akhtīj festival, at the opening of the farming season at the close of the annual rains, the Bhīls marry, in the form of two wooden dolls, the deities who control the rains, and as soon as the rains come, they throw these images into a stream.[6]

When these aboriginal cults are taken over by the Brāhmans, the rite of the sacred marriage becomes rapidly

[1] *Journal Anthropological Society*, Bombay, ii. 269, vii. 637, 642; F. R. Hemingway, *Gazetteer Godāvarī District*, i. 48; Bishop Whitehead, *op. cit.* 18.

[2] [Sir] E. Gait, *Census Report, Bengal*, 1901, i. 187, 188, 190, 191, 193.

[3] *Ibid.* 189; E. T. Dalton, *Descriptive Ethnology of Bengal*, 261; P. Dehon, *Memoirs Asiatic Society of Bengal*, i. 145.

[4] *Popular Religion and Folklore of Northern India*, 2nd ed. ii. 322 *et seqq.*

[5] S. C. Macpherson, *Memorials of Service in India*, 84.

[6] C. E. Luard, *Ethnographical Survey, Central India*, Art. *Bhīl*, p. 29.

developed. Mr. F. J. Richards, who has made a special study of Dravidian religious beliefs, informs me that, in his opinion, most cases of the sacred marriage in Southern India are due to Brāhman influence. Thus, Mīnādchī, "Fish Rule," the Tanjore goddess, a true Dravidian deity, is now married to Siva.[1] Some of the goddesses of the Meithei tribe are married, but this, too, seems to be a Brāhman rite.[2] The goddess Tulasī, the impersonation of the sacred basil plant, is married annually in Kāthiāwār to Vishnu, or to his embodiment in the sacred ammonite, the Sālagrāma.[3] The same goddess in the Bhandāra District of the Central Provinces is married to the Sālagrāma: sugar-cane, onions, garlic, and wild plums, from which the people abstained during her four months' sleep, are offered to her and then eaten.[4] In the Bījāpur District the goddess Pārvatī is annually married to Sangameswar, the presiding deity of the sacred river junction.[5] We reach a lower animistic stage in the marriage of the goddess Dyamavvā in the Dharwār District to the holy sacrificial buffalo, which represents her husband, a man of the menial Mahār caste.[6] In the northern plains we meet with few cases of this kind, or they are obscured by elaborate Brahmanical rites, but in the Himālaya, at the Nandashtami festival held in the month Bhādon during the rainy season, the hill Mother Nandā or Pārvatī is solemnly wedded to Siva.[7] The rites of the sacred marriage form a favourite

[1] Thurston, *op. cit.* iii. 85; *Madras Manual of Administration*, iii. 499.

[2] T. C. Hodson, *The Meitheis*, 97 *et seq.*

[3] *Bombay Gazetteer*, vii. 527, viii. 667.

[4] R. V. Russell, *Gazetteer Bhandāra District*, i. 49.

[5] *Bombay Gazetteer*, xxiii. 676.

[6] *Ibid.* xxii. 810. For this sacred buffalo, called Devarā Potū, see Bishop Whitehead, *op. cit.* 88.

[7] E. T. Atkinson, *op. cit.* ii. 792. For a full account of the sacred marriage, see Sir J. G. Frazer, *The Golden Bough*, 3rd ed. *The Magic Art*, ii. 120 *et seqq.*

subject of Indian art: for instance, it is represented, in the case of Siva and Pārvatī in the Caves of Elephanta.[1]

The Mana of the Mothers is also reinforced or restored by blood sacrifice, especially of a male victim, whose shivering, stimulated by pouring water on its back, indicates that it is possessed by the deity, when it is slain at once by a single stroke, in order to prevent the Mana from being dispersed and lost.[2] But it is still believed that unless the victim is subjected to torture or meets with a tedious death, the state of tension requisite for the accumulation and bestowal of the Mana will not be attained. Hence we find that the animal is ill-treated, beaten, crushed, or trampled to death, preventing the careless effusion of blood which is the prime vehicle of the Mana. Such barbarities are a scandal in the popular ritual.[3]

It is impossible to discuss in detail the question whether this type of sacrifice is communal or not; the theory that it corresponds to the Semitic type of sacrifice is supported by Bishop Whitehead, but his remarks do not carry complete conviction.[4] There are certainly points of resemblance:—the meat is cooked by the men of the menial castes who perform the rite, and it is eaten there and then before the god, except the head, the share of the officiant, which he usually takes to his home: as a general rule none of the flesh may be removed from the sacred place. This last precaution may imply nothing more than that the flesh is regarded as sacrosanct or tabu, and it is a fact that many high castes, like the Nāmbūtiri Brahmans of Malabar, the most conservative of Hindus, who aim at

[1] J. Fergusson, J. Burgess, *The Cave Temples of India*, 471; V. A. Smith, *History of Fine Art in India and Ceylon*, 215, with a photograph.

[2] See M. Haug, *Essays on the Sacred Language, Writings, and Religion of the Parsis*, 128.

[3] See the remarks on Hausa sacrifices, A. J. N. Tremearne, *The Ban of the Borī*, 239 f. On the mysterious power of blood, A. A. Macdonell, A. B. Keith, *Vedic Index*, ii. 146.

[4] *Op. cit.* 144.

following the ancient Vedic rites, never eat meat except that of a sacrificed victim.[1] The use of the sacred rice of Jagannāth by the Kandhs seem to be sacramental. But sacrifice in India usually takes the form of a gift to the god, for which in return material benefits are expected, and the evidence for the existence of the communal type is not quite convincing.

The latest and most objectionable phase of Mother worship is Saktism, the worship of the active female principle (prakriti), as manifested in the goddesses, consorts of Siva.[2]

The account of Mother worship here given is merely a sketch of an extremely complex subject, regarding which our knowledge is still defective. Much has been done to elucidate it by Bishop Whitehead, Mr. F. J. Richards, and other writers, principally for southern India. It may be hoped that the outlines which I have given will stimulate further inquiry, and provide further information which may throw much-needed light on the special developments of the cultus in Crete, Early Greece, and Western Asia.

[1] *Vishnu Parāna*, iii. 11, trans. H. H. Wilson, 1840, p. 307; Manu, *Laws*, v. 7; *Bombay Gazetteer*, xviii. 51; Thurston, *op. cit.* v. 235; E. W. Hopkins, *op. cit.* 185 note, 288 note. "In the Vedic texts no Kshatriya can eat of the sacrificial offering (*Aitareya Brāhmana*, vii. 26), no doubt because only the Brāhmanas were sufficiently holy to receive the divine essence of the sacrifice into which, by partaking of it, the deity has entered in part" (A. A. Macdonell, A. B. Keith, *Vedic Index*, i. 112, ii. 83, 145).

[2] N. Macnicol, *Indian Theism from the Vedic to the Muhammadan Period*, 180 *et seqq.*: Hopkins, *op. cit.* 489 *et seqq.*; A. Avalon, *Tantra of the Great Liberation*, *Hymns to the Goddess*, *Principles of Tantra.*

SOME NOTES ON HOMERIC FOLK-LORE.

BY W. CROOKE.

(*Read at Meeting, 15th May*, 1907.)

IN this paper I propose to deal with some of the folk-lore and folk-tales to be found in the Homeric poems, and it is not my intention to join, except indirectly, the mellay of the Unitarians,—those who, like Mr. Lang, contend that the *Iliad* and *Odyssey* are the work of a single writer,—and the Separatists, or, as they used to be called, the Chorizontes, represented by Mr. Leaf. But the study of the folk-lore and folk-tales of Homer is so closely connected with the problem of origins that it is impossible to pass by this controversy in silence.

As students of tradition and romance our sympathies are probably on the side of the old-fashioned view which attributes both epics to a single writer. The arguments in its favour have been forcibly stated by Mr. Lang in his recent book.[1] In the first place, he has made a well-timed protest against the "analytical reader," "the literary entomologist," as he has recently been profanely called. "The poet," he justly remarks, "is expected to satisfy a minutely critical reader, a personage whom he could not foresee, and whom he did not address." He accepts the statement of Mr. Leaf that the epics were "Court poems. They were composed to be sung in the

[1] *Homer and his Age*, in continuation of his earlier work, *Homer and the Epic*.

palaces of a ruling aristocracy . . . the poems are aristocratic and courtly"; they are in no sense ballads or folk-song. This fact, as will be suggested later on, tends to explain some curious omissions, and the reticence which the poet displays regarding ideas and traditions which must have been within his knowledge. Any one who has had personal experience of such Court poets, like the Bhâts, who are the singers and panegyrists of the aristocracy of India, will easily understand why the poems contain the inconsistencies on which the Separatists have laid special stress. It is most improbable that the epics were reduced to writing in the age during which they were composed, and it seems quite certain that the audience which heard portions of them recited in the great hall of a palace troubled itself little about the contradictions which impress the modern critic, even if these attracted attention.

Mr. Lang, again, has done good service in showing that the *Iliad* has a well-developed plot, and he adduces weighty arguments to prove that the Doloneia, or Tenth Book, forms a necessary part of it. He also, with much ingenuity, displays the consistency of the character of Agamemnon throughout the *Iliad*. He argues that both epics represent the culture, customs, and art of a single age. In particular, the methods of disposal of the dead have supplied large materials for controversy. This question seems to be placed out of court by his remark that the people of Australia and Tasmania practise, or did practise, every conceivable way of disposing of their dead.[1] I have lately had occasion to consider this question with special reference to India. Here we find no uniformity of practice. Inhumation, cairn burial, crouched burial, burial in shaft graves, exposure to beasts and birds, disposal on platforms, and various forms of cremation, are some of the many modes which prevail

[1] *Homer and his Age*, 95.

among tribes not ethnically distinct, and possessing a fairly uniform degree of culture. Further, we find these customs varying under our very eyes—forest tribes who used to bury their dead adopting cremation when they come under Brahman influence, and Hindus converted to Islam or Christianity replacing cremation by inhumation. Rites of this kind, in short, seem to be liable to constant modification, and provide no safe criterion for deciding the relative ages of poems like the epics.

The facts thus collected seem to indicate unity of age and authorship of the *Iliad*. The relation of the *Iliad* to the *Odyssey* is a much more difficult question. I do not pretend to offer an opinion on the arguments based on archaeology and philology; but I am inclined to think that the linguistic differences in the two poems, of which a catalogue has been prepared by that great scholar, Mr. Munro, have not been fully met by Mr. Lang. From the point of view of religion, again, Professor Lewis Campbell has given a long list of the "obvious differences" between the standpoint of the two poems;[1] and the same view has been adopted by Professor Gilbert Murray,[2] both critics being deeply impressed by the splendour of Homer's poetry. Mr. Lang's main answer to these arguments seems to be that they do not fit in with Mr. Leaf's scheme of breaking up the *Iliad* into "cantos."[3] Another set of arguments against the unity of the two poems has been produced by Mr. Hall,[4] who points out that whereas in the *Iliad* the Dorians are of no account among the Greek tribes, in the *Odyssey* they appear to have reached the end of their migrations; that in the *Iliad* the process of the withdrawal of the Phoenicians from the Aegean seems to have begun, in the *Odyssey* they appear to have disappeared from Greece, and

[1] *Religion in Greek Literature*, 84 ff.

[2] *History of Ancient Greek Literature*, 33 ff. [3] *Op. cit.* 231 f.

[4] *The Oldest Civilisation of Greece*, 42, 236, 246, 258, 269.

are found trading more especially outside Greek waters; that the knowledge of Italy shown in the *Odyssey* points to a later date; and that local politics in the Egyptian delta fix the date of the raid of Odysseus[1] at the end of the eighth or the beginning of the seventh century B.C.

Mr. Lang is at his best in demonstrating that the schemes for the dislocation of the *Iliad* into lays are impracticable and self-contradictory. The Separatist theory, in short, involves at least two serious difficulties: first, that, assuming the Menis or Wrath of Achilles, the "kernel" of the poem, as Mr. Leaf calls it, to be the work of a writer whom we may call Homer, there must have been, in or about the same age, at least two or three equally great poets who were content to merge their personalities in his, or were identified with him; secondly, that if the present arrangement of the epic is the work of a later editor, it is a mystery how a writer of such genius as his must have been could have left the discrepancies and difficulties which at once attract the attention of the modern critic. The result of the whole investigation seems to be that we may provisionally accept the *Iliad*, with certain later additions, as the work of a single hand, while the *Odyssey* probably comes from a different and later writer. "The poems," says Professor Campbell, "are a treasure-house of things new and old, preserving some relics of an immemorial past like flies in amber, while bearing on their surface all the gloss of novelty."[2]

In studying part of the large mass of literature devoted to this controversy it occurred to me that if arguments for and against the unity of the epics can be based on considerations like those of armour, the use of bronze and iron, customs of disposal of the dead, and similar considerations to which Mr. Lang's recent book is largely devoted, it might be possible to apply a similar test

[1] *Od.* xiv. 259. [2] *Op. cit.* 54.

dependent on the provenience of the Sagas, Märchen, and folk-lore incidents which appear in the poems. If, for instance, the "kernel" of the *Iliad* was composed on Greek soil, and was subsequently extended by an Ionic poet, we would expect that some indications of this would appear in the folk-lore. So that if taking the scheme of arrangement of the "cantos" in the *Iliad*, as proposed by Mr. Leaf, and comparing these with the *Odyssey* we could show that there is anything like a stratification of belief or tradition, and that this corresponds with the suggested divisions of the poems, we should have an argument of some importance in disproof of the unity of authorship. I hope that in making this investigation I shall not lay myself open to the sarcastic comment of a recent writer, who, reviewing the work of the Separatists, remarks that "we feel as if we were assisting at the midnight adulteration of some new brand of sugar behind a grocer's counter."[1] I trust that the reverence in which I hold the poems will save me from such a charge. In considering the folk-lore and folk tales I shall comment occasionally on any result of this scrutiny which seems of any value, leaving the references in the notes to this paper to speak for themselves. I may say at once that the investigation, for reasons which I will suggest later on, has led to no definite result.[2]

To return to the sources of the poems—attempts have also been made to discriminate the evidence of foreign influence, of the knowledge of savagery and of lands beyond the Hellenic area, which appears in the epics. For instance, in the *Iliad* alone we find a reference

[1] *Edinburgh Review*, cci. 210.

[2] The references follow Leaf's scheme as given in his *Iliad*, 1st ed. In the 2nd ed. he gives a similar, but less elaborate classification. i. represents the Menis or "kernel" of the poem; ii. A, ii. B, ii. C, the "Earlier Expansions"; iii. the "Later Expansions"; iv. the "Greater Interpolations; v. "Short Interpolated Passages by which the transitions from one piece to another of different ages were managed."

to the Pheres, probably some aboriginal race; and the writer seems to display special knowledge of the Thracian tribes.[1] The *Odyssey* is said to show a wider outlook in the direction of Sicily and Italy; but it exhibits no extension of knowledge towards the Propontis and Euxine, while the information possessed by the writer of the *Iliad* of the Troad and of the peoples of Asia Minor is no longer to be traced.[2] On the other hand, the *Iliad* knows of the Central African Pygmies, and the tale of the Laestrygonians in the *Odyssey* seems to point to an acquaintance with the Vikings or their predecessors of northern Europe. How far this may be due to the difference of subject in the two poems is a question for careful consideration.

Marks of Semitic influence, again, have been traced in the epics. An instance of this will be suggested later on in connexion with the Saga of Bellerophon. To this source has also been attributed the reference to the rainbow as a sign;[3] that to Iris as a winged goddess, unique in the poems;[4] the mention of a flood as a punishment for wickedness;[5] and of the palm tree at Delos.[6] It has been the habit to attribute Homer's knowledge of Western Mediterranean folk-tales, like those of the Cyclops and Atlas, to Phoenician influence. But it is now certain that the Mycenaean culture was of home growth, and that it cannot be assigned to a non-Greek race, like the Phoenicians. The connexion of the Phoenicians with the Persian Gulf is now generally discredited;[7] and from the Tel-el-Amarna records it is clear that as early as 1400 B.C. Babylon was the dominant power in Western Asia, and that its civilisation passed

[1] *Il.* i. 268 [i.]; ii. 743 [iv.]; Geddes, *Problem of the Homeric Poems*, 69, 244.

[2] Monro, *Odyssey*, ii. 337.

[3] *Il.* xi. 28; xvii. 548: [both in v.].

[4] *Il.* viii. 398 [iii. B].

[5] *Il.* xvi. 384 f. [v.].

[6] *Od.* vi. 162.

[7] Hogarth, *Journal Anthropological Institute*, xxxii. 349.

into the Aegean independent of Phoenician agency. The discoveries in Crete, again, imply the existence of a great sea power in the Aegean as early perhaps as the second millennium before Christ; and in this way the sites which, according to M. Bérard, were associated with the Märchen of the *Odyssey*—the city of Alcinous in a west Corfiote site, the island of Calypso in that of Peregil near Ceuta, the cave of the Cyclops at Cumae—must have become known to the Greeks at a period much earlier than is usually supposed, and independently of information from Phoenician mariners.

Again, in dealing with the question of Semitic influence on early Greek beliefs, it must not be forgotten that, as Mr. A. J. Evans points out,[1] while it may be admitted that it may have left traces, as Egypt certainly did, on the externals of Mycenaean worship, there was an underlying race-connexion between the pre-Hellenic population of Greece and its islands and the Anatolian region. "The pure Semite is, in fact, difficult to find in Anatolia or Palestine," and "in Cilicia and northern Syria he has largely assimilated elements belonging to that old Anatolian stock of which the Carians and the Cilicians stand out as the leading representatives, and which was itself linked on by island stepping-stones to pre-historic Greece." The suggestion, then, of direct borrowing from oriental sources must be reconsidered in the light of recent historical and ethnographical research.

In dealing with folk-tradition in the epics nothing is perhaps more remarkable than what may be called the reticence of the poet. A singer of lays before a courtly audience, he knows that his hearers will take little interest in the rude peasant cults. Dionysus he regards as an outsider, received with hostility, and if he was the successor of a village god the poet makes no mention of him. If Homer was a native of the Greek mainland he must have

[1] *Journal Hellenic Studies*, xxi. 131.

been familiar with the coarse archaic cults, which are embalmed for us in the pages of Pausanias, but he carefully avoids all mention of them. Demeter is referred to in the *Iliad*, but she hardly ranks as an Olympian goddess. She is spoken of as the wife or mistress of Zeus; but there is no mention of a child born to the pair, and only once, in the *Odyssey*, is a personal legend told of her, when she yields to her love of Iason, and lies with him in the thrice-ploughed field[1]—"one of the lovely earth-born myths that crop up now and again in Homer, telling of an older simpler world, of gods who had only half emerged from the natural things they are, real earth-born flesh-and-blood creatures, not splendid phantoms of an imagined Olympian pageant."[2] As the Indian Sītā sprang from a furrow, we recognise in the myth the familiar story of the Sacred Marriage, which attributed to the union of the Earth goddess with her male partner, the fertility of the soil. The representation of this in dramatic form was an important incident in the Mysteries, and was described in a passage of splendid poetical imagination, where Hera beguiles Zeus to couch with her on the crest of Gargaros.[3]

It is equally remarkable that we have no mention of the serpent cult. We have two snake portents, the snake devouring the sparrows and the bird bearing a snake;[4] a snake of cyanus adorns the breastplate of Agamemnon;[5] we hear of a dragon fed on poisonous herbs, of a deadly water-snake, and Alexandros starts back as one who sees a serpent in a mountain glade.[6] But of a snake cult we hear nothing, and this in spite of the fact that it might have been connected with two personages to whom the

[1] *Od.* v. 125.

[2] Miss Harrison, *Prolegomena to the Study of Greek Religion*, 566.

[3] *Il.* xiv. 296 ff. [iii.]; Farnell, *Cults of the Greek States*, i. 184 ff.

[4] *Il.* ii. 308 ff. [ii. A]; xii. 200 ff. [iii.]. [5] *Il.* xi. 26 f. [v.].

[6] *Il.* xxii. 93 f. [i.]; ii. 723 [iv.]; iii. 33 f. [ii. B].

poet refers. He knows of Erechtheus, to whom Athene gave a resting-place in her rich sanctuary.[1] But both he and Pausanias are reticent about the sacred serpent which, according to Herodotus, abode there.[2] He also knows of Asklepios, the great healer, who in his view is not a deity, but a man with mortal sons who learned their craft from him, and he is called "the blameless leech," an epithet never applied to a god.[3] And yet the poet says nothing of his snake, although, as Dr. Frazer shows,[4] it is tolerably certain that Asklepios was originally nothing more or less than a serpent, which at a later time was transformed into an anthropomorphic figure with a serpent symbol.

It is equally remarkable that the poet carefully selects certain legends for treatment and discards others. His silence, in short, means nothing in connexion with his knowledge of cultus or folk-lore. In some cases doubtless the legend was developed after his time by the later epic writers and tragedians. But he certainly knew some of the stories although he pays little attention to them. Thus of the famous tale of Jason and the Argonauts he tells us little, except in one passage in the *Odyssey*.[5] While relating the legend of the Symplegades or Wandering Rocks, he mentions incidentally that only one ship of all that sail on the sea, even Argo that is in the minds of all, ever passed that way; and even her the waves would have cast upon the mighty rocks had not Hera, for love of Jason, passed her through. We are told, again, that Euneus, whom Hypsipyle bore to Jason, supplied the Achaeans with wine, and it was apparently he who bought Lykaon as a slave, and the ransom of Lykaon was the silver cup which he gave to Patroclus.[6] Of Medea there is no record in the poems, unless she be identical with Agamede, the daughter of Augeias, who, like Medea, was a grand-daughter of Helios,

[1] *Il.* ii. 547 [iv.]; *Od.* vii. 81.
[2] *Pausanias*, i. 26, 5; *Herod.* viii. 41.
[3] *Il.* ii. 731 [iv.]; iv. 194 [ii. B]; xi. 518 [i.].
[4] *Pausanias*, iii. 65 f.
[5] xii. 69 ff.
[6] *Il.* vii. 467 ff. [iii.], xxi. 41 [i.], xxiii. 747 [iv.].

and knew all the drugs which the wide earth nurtureth.[1] At any rate Homer does not connect her with the Argonauts; and this was probably a later expansion of the legend. If the poet was familiar with the tale, it is strange that he does not refer to it; for it abounds in excellent epic material. Thus the incident of the cauldron in which she induced the daughters of Pelias to boil their father in order to restore his youth appears in European folk-lore in the story where Christ or St. Peter, or the Devil, wanders through the world in disguise, and restores an old man to youth or a dead person to life by boiling him in a kettle or roasting him in a forge; a bungler, generally a blacksmith, tries to perform the same trick and fails.[2] Like this is the Indian tale of Chyavana, who is restored to youth by bathing under the advice of the Asvins, and the wide cycle connected with the Well of Life, which revives even the ashes of the dead.[3] There is, again, in the Medea Saga, the fatal wedding-robe which consumes the bridegroom, and this in the German story is made of sulphur and pitch.[4] The yoking of the fire-breathing bulls and the sowing of the dragon's teeth appear in the Kalevala in the form of the field of serpents which Ilmarinen must plough before he can win his bride.[5] Lastly, Medea's slaughter of the children points to the fact that she is originally a divinity, probably of Semitic origin, closely associated with Hera, and that the sacrifice of children was part of the archaic ritual at her shrine.[6]

Of the famous tale of Philoktetes, again, Homer tells us only that he lay in sore pain at Lemnos, where the

[1] *Il.* xi. 740 [iv.].

[2] Grimm, *Household Tales*, i. 312 f.; Ralston, *Russian Folk Tales*, 57 f.; Crane, *Italian Popular Tales*, 188 f.; Frazer, *Pausanias*, iv. 218; *Adonis, Attis, Osiris*, 93.

[3] Knowles, *Folk Tales of Kashmir*, 504. [4] Grimm, *Household Tales*, i. 23 f.

[5] *Kalevala*, Rune 19; Frazer, *op. cit.* iii. 26; Rhys, *Hibbert Lectures*, 291.

[6] Farnell, *op. cit.* i. 203; Frazer, *op. cit.* iii. 26 f.

Achaeans left him sick of a grievous wound from a deadly water snake; that he returned home in safety, and that he alone surpassed Odysseus in archery.[1] Though the use of poisoned arrows was familiar to the poet, we do not hear of them in connexion with the hero.

So with Melampus, a notable figure in Greek folk-lore, who was endowed with prophetic power, who first practised the art of medicine and established the cult of Dionysus in Greece. Of him the poet records two different traditions;[2] but we are not told that he knew the language of birds, and that he was warned to leave his house by hearing the wood-worms say that the roof-beam was well nigh eaten through. In this he resembles the Norse Heimdall, who had an ear so fine that he could hear the grass growing in the meadows and the wool on the backs of the sheep. The same tale of semi-divine prescience of coming disaster is told of Gauhar Shah, a modern Hindu saint.[3]

There is perhaps no tale better adapted to romantic treatment than that of Admetus and his devoted wife, Alkestis. But of her all we learn from Homer is that she was fair among women, the most lovely of the daughters of Pelias, and bore Eumelus, the charioteer to Admetus.[4] We hear nothing of Oenone, or of the Apples of the Hesperides, which appear in Celtic legend and in the Arabic tale of Ala-ud-din.[5] Lastly, Homer tells us little of Herakles, save that many labours were imposed upon him by a man inferior to himself. We learn only of the fetching of the Dog of the Underworld, which the poet does not name.[6] And yet Herakles has a widespread

[1] *Il.* ii. 716 ff. [iv.]; *Od.* iii. 190, viii. 219.

[2] *Od.* xi. 281 ff., xv. 225 ff.

[3] Mallet, *Northern Antiquities*, 95; Crooke, *Popular Religion and Folk-lore of N. India*, i. 190.

[4] *Il.* ii. 713 f. [iv.], xxiii. 532 f. [iv.].

[5] Jacobs, *Celtic Fairy Tales*, 244; Burton, *Arabian Nights* (Library ed.), x. 50.

[6] *Od.* xi. 621 f.

cultus as a god of dreams and of warm springs, as a worm-slayer, the counterpart of the Semitic Melkart.[1]

The best explanation of such omissions is found in what Professor Raleigh says of Shakespeare, a kindred genius: "Plays like those of Shakespeare cannot be written in cold blood; they call forth the man's whole energies, and take toll of the last farthing of his wealth of sympathy and experience. In the plays we may learn what are the questions that interest Shakespeare most profoundly and recur to his mind with most insistence; we may note how he handles his story, what he rejects and what he alters, changing its purport and fashion; how many points he is content to leave dark; what matters he chooses to decorate with the highest resources of his dramatic art, and what he gives over to be the sport of triumphant ridicule; how in every type of character he emphasises what most appeals to his instinct and imagination, so that we see the meaning of character more plainly than it is to be seen in life . . . how dare we complain that he has hidden himself from our knowledge?"[2]

Let us now consider some of the folk-lore in the epics. In dealing with Homeric Animism it is hard to say how much represents actual belief and how much metaphor; and its occurrence in what are supposed to be the oldest portion of the poems may be due to the superior energy and imagination of the older writer. Thus, a stone is called "stubborn" or "relentless" in not quite the earliest portions of the *Iliad*, and also in the *Odyssey*.[3] At times a distinctly human emotion is ascribed to inanimate nature: the earth laughs or groans, the sea rejoices or rouses the Argives, in the earliest as well as in the latest cantos.[4] The river Scamander waxes wroth in heart in the "kernel"

[1] *Pausanias*, ii. 35, 5; Müller, *Dorians* (E.T.) i. 373; Frazer, *Adonis, Attis, Osiris*, 12, 35, 41, 118 ff.

[2] *Shakespeare*, 8. [3] *Il.* iv. 521 [ii. A], xiii. 139 [ii. C]; *Od.* xi. 598.

[4] *Il.* xix. 362 [i.], xiii. 29 [iii.], xxi. 357 [iv.], xiv. 392 [v.].

of the *Iliad,* but speaks with a voice out of the whirlpool in one of the later lays.[1] In the same fashion waves and shores bellow, and the sea is prescient of a storm.[2] The belief in birth from rocks and trees, which is probably mere rhetoric, appears twice in the *Menis,* once in the *Odyssey.*[3] Lastly, it is impossible to detect any stratification in the mention of weapons craving for slaughter, which is often quoted as an instance of Animism.[4] In the *Ramayana* "the great bow embossed with gold Throbs eager for the master's hold."[5] The spears of the Irish Red Branch champions, we are told, "were regularly seized with the rage for massacre; and then the bronze head grew red-hot, so that it had to be kept in a caldron of cold water, or, more commonly, of black poisonous liquid, into which it was plunged whenever it blazed up with the murder fit."[6]

To take the cases in which supernatural intelligence and powers of speech are attributed to animals.—Though the horse Arion is mentioned in the *Iliad,*[7] the crude legend of its birth from Demeter and its powers of reason and speech are ignored.[8] But we have other instances of these gifted beasts. Antilochus, Achilles, and Menelaus appeal to their horses, and Polyphemus to his ram, throughout the epics,[9] and the horses of Achilles weep in sympathy with their lord.[10] This communion of man and beast is common in folk-lore, and the power of understanding beast language is gained in various ways—by eating porridge mixed with

[1] xxi. 136 f. [i.], xxi. 413 [iv.].

[2] xvii. 265 [i.], ii. 210, iv. 425 [ii. A], xiv. 17 [iii.], xiv. 394 [v.].

[3] *Il.* xvi. 34, xxii. 126 [i.]; *Od.* xix. 162 f.

[4] *Il.* xi. 574, xxi. 70 [i.], iv. 125 [ii. B], xv. 317 [iii.], xxi. 168 [iv.].

[5] Griffith, *Ramayan,* 256. [6] Joyce, *Social History of Ancient Ireland,* i. 114.

[7] xxiii. 346 [v.]. [8] *Pausanias,* viii. 25, 4, with Frazer's note.

[9] *Il.* xxiii. 402 ff. [iv.], xix. 399 ff. [i.], viii. 184 ff. [iii. B]; *Od.* xv. 150 ff., ix. 446 ff.

[10] *Il.* xvii. 426 ff. [ii. C].

the slaver of tortured snakes, by Finn's broiled fish and Sigfried's roasted dragon's heart, or by eating a white snake or a herb like a fern.[1] With these gifted horses which speak and lament the fate of their owner we may compare the Karling legend of Bayard, and Skirnir in the *Edda* talking to his horse, as Godrun does with Grani after the murder of Sigurd.[2] In Persian myth the same power is attributed to the steed of Rustum; in an Irish story the ram speaks to St. Magnenn, as in a Kashmir tale the horse warns his master, the Raja, against his treacherous Wazir; and in the Hindu tale of Vidhusaka, the hero, seeing no means of escape from his trouble, and knowing what his horse had been in a previous birth, bows before him and says: "Thou art a god; a creature like thee cannot commit treason against his lord." On which appeal the horse obeys his master, "for excellent horses are divine beings."[3]

Another of these sacred Homeric beasts is the boar, which the offended Artemis sends against the garden land of Oineus.[4] This reminds us of the mythic swine of Ireland, reared with malice and venom that it might be the bane of the men of Erinn, or the Erymanthian boar slain by Herakles.[5]

Again, to take the cult of trees—A phrase employed by Homer implies that the earliest temple was a booth of branches,[6] and it has been supposed that the same idea is involved in the custom of hanging up the arms of defeated combatants, which appears in the second canto of the *Iliad* as well as in the *Odyssey*.[7] In the same canto of the

[1] Elton-Powell, *Saxo*, Intro. lxix.; Miss Cox, *Cinderella*, 496 ff.

[2] Grimm, *Teutonic Mythology* [E.T.], i. 392.

[3] Clouston, *Popular Tales*, i. 45 f.; O'Grady, *Silva Gadelica*, ii. 37; Knowles, *Folk Tales of Kashmir*, 353; Tawney, *Katha Sarit Sagara*, i. 130.

[4] *Il.* ix. 533 ff. [iv.].

[5] Rhys, *Hibbert Lectures*, 511; *id. Celtic Folk-lore*, ii. 509 f.

[6] *Il.* i. 39 [i.].

[7] *Il.* v. 82 f. [ii. A]; *Od.* iii. 274 f.

E

Iliad we find a reference to the very archaic belief in the grave-tree as an abode for the spirit of the dead man, when the mountain Nymphs plant elm-trees round the barrow of Aetion.[1] A similar tale is told of Protesilaus, round whose barrow elm-trees grew; those which faced towards Troy bloomed early and withering fell untimely, like the hero himself, and of Geryon, on whose grave the trees dropped blood.[2] We have the same idea in the folk-tales of the grave-trees springing from the corpse and becoming a refuge for the spirit.

> "Margaret was buryed in the lower chancel,
> And William in the higher:
> Out of her breast there sprang a rose,
> And out of his a briar."[3]

In Samoa the grave of a chief is called "the house thatched with the leaves of the sandal-wood," in allusion to the custom of planting some tree with pretty foliage near the grave.[4] So in the Celtic tale of Baile and Ailinn the yew and apple trees grew from the lovers' graves and when cut down were made into tablets on which the poets inscribed their pitiful story.[5] It is only in the *Odyssey* that we have a vague hint of the equally archaic belief in the birth-tree, if the palm springing at the altar of Apollo which Odysseus saw, refers to the birth-palm under which Leto was delivered.[6]

It seems equally impossible to discover any stratification of the more primitive religious beliefs in the *Iliad.* Perhaps the most archaic cultus recorded in the poems is that of Dodonaean Zeus. It is at the supreme crisis

[1] *Il.* vi. 419 f. [ii. A]. [2] Frazer, *Pausanias*, ii. 473, 483.

[3] "Fair Margaret and Sweet William," Percy, *Ballads*, ed. Wheatley, iii. 126.

[4] Miss Stokes, *Indian Fairy Tales*, 244, 250 f.; Turner, *Samoa*, 147.

[5] Joyce, *Social History*, i. 481 f.

[6] *Od.* vi. 162 f.; *Pausanias*, viii. 4, 7; Plutarch, *De Iside*, 15; Grimm, *Household Tales*, i. 187.

when Achilles sends Patroclus to the fight that he invokes him :

> "who dwell'st remote, O Zeus supreme !
> The lord of all Pelasgos, and enthroned
> On frore Dodona's snows ; and round thy throne
> Circle the Sellian seers, for thee devote
> To feet unwashen, and to bed the earth."[1]

This is in the *Menis*, but the other two references to Dodona are found in the *Odyssey*.[2] At Dodona, according to Professor Ridgeway, occurred the first clash of Pelasgian and Achaean, and here Zeus and his shadow-wife, Dione, displaced the old Earth Mother and her dove priestesses.[3] Hence we find here a dove cult, which in its earliest stages had no connexion with Aphrodite, but with Zeus, to whom in another passage the doves bring nectar.[4] Again, we find at Dodona that Odysseus visits the oracular tree, to learn the counsels of Zeus from the high leafy oak-tree of the god. The notice of this archaic cultus is found not in the *Iliad*, but in the *Odyssey*.[5] Aeschylus speaks of these prophetic oaks of Dodona, Sophocles of the oak of many voices, and Herodotus tells how "two black doves flew away from Egyptian Thebes, and on alighting at the Dodona oak began to speak with human voice and told them that on this spot should be the oracle of Zeus."[6] Such oracular trees, like the burning bush of Moses, the "tree of the augurs," near Shechem, the oak of Moreh, the palm tree of Deborah, are common in the beliefs of the Semites and other races.[7] Thirdly,

[1] *Il.* xvi. 233 ff. [i.]. [2] xiv. 327, xix. 296.

[3] Ridgeway, *Early Age of Greece*, i. 339; Miss Harrison, *Prolegomena*, 334.

[4] *Od.* xii. 62 f.; A. J. Evans, *Journal Hellenic Studies*, xxi. 105.

[5] *Od.* xiv. 327 f.; xix. 296 f.

[6] Aesch. *Prom. Vinct.* 851 ; Soph. *Trach.* 1168 ; *Herod.* ii. 55.

[7] Robertson Smith, *Religion of the Semites*,[2] 194 ; A. J. Evans, *Journal Hellenic Studies*, xxi. 133 ; *Folk-lore*, xv. 295 ; *Journal Anthropological Institute*, xxx. 36 ; cf. the ancient Irish divination with branches of the sacred yew, Joyce, *op. cit.* i. 230.

the priests of this pre-Hellenic god were subject to various taboos. Thus, they were obliged to sleep on the ground, as is the rule with the chief priest of Zinda Kaliāna in the Panjab, who must sleep on the ground or on a square bed of grass made on the earth between four posts, a form of primitive asceticism, the idea that ghosts cannot touch the ground possibly aiding in the establishment of the practice.[1] For the same reason the votaries of Sultān in the Panjab sleep on the ground, not on a bedstead; and in memory, it is said, of the fall of their capital, Chithor, but more probably in obedience to some primitive taboo, the old Rajputs used vessels of clay instead of metal, and slept on straw, while the modern Raja, though he eats off gold and silver, and sleeps on a bed, places leaves beneath the one and straw under the other.[2] Apparently for the same reason the Roman Flamen Dialis had the feet of his bed smeared with mud, and the priest of the old Prussian god, Potrimpo, was bound to sleep on the bare earth for three days before he performed sacrifice.[3]

The custom of the Selloi keeping their feet unwashed presents more difficulty. We have many cases in which the removal of foot-gear in holy places is prescribed, as in the Semitic ritual, probably lest the shoes might become taboo and unfit for future use by contact with the holy ground.[4] The officiant at the Latin Lemuria walked barefoot through the house, possibly on the theory that he thus was unfettered, and there was a special Roman rite, the Nudipedalia, in which barefooted matrons walked in procession in order to prevent drought; while the Egyptian priests, like the modern Kafirs of North India, took off their shoes at the time of sacrifice.[5] At

[1] Rose, *Punjab Census Report*, 1901, i. 118 f.

[2] *North Indian Notes and Queries*, iv. 59.

[3] Frazer, *Classical Review*, ii. 322; *id. Golden Bough*,[2] i. 242.

[4] Robertson Smith, *op. cit.* 453.

[5] Fowler, *Roman Festivals*, 109; Conder, *Tent Life in Palestine*, ii. 221;

the Inibe, or rite of abstinence in Japan, the medicine-man was not allowed to comb his hair, eat meat, or approach women, and if his clients fell ill they set it down to his failure to keep his vows.[1] In the case of the Selloi the rule of keeping the feet unwashed may be a survival of some primitive ascetic ritual, as the Hindu Faqir smears himself with dust or ashes to indicate to all and sundry that he is in a state of taboo, and this may have attracted the attention of the later Greeks by its startling contrast to the elaborate rules of personal purity which marked the officiants of the service of the Olympian gods.[2]

It is remarkable that the shadowy Dione, the partner of the older Zeus, is mentioned only once in the epics, and that not in the "kernel," but in one of the so-called later additions.[3]

Two primitive forms of oath appear in the poems—one in connexion with animal victims; the other by the river Styx. The former does not occur, as perhaps we might have expected, in the older cantos.[4] The conception of Styx varies in Homer. By one account it is a stream of this world, or at least closely connected with it, because the Titaresios of Thessaly is a branch of it; by another it is a river of the underworld, and a branch of it is Cocytus; elsewhere it is described as a waterfall.[5] This oath by Styx is undoubtedly a most primitive rite. In the first place, Dr. Frazer has shown that the fact that a draught of its water is considered deadly, points to the conclusion that it originally represented one of those poison ordeals

Maspero, *Dawn of Civilisation*, 124; Robertson, *Kafirs of the Hindu-Kush*, 429; Newton, *Essays on Art and Archaeology*, 156, 178.

[1] Aston, *Nihongi*, i. 42 n.

[2] Hall's view is that the Selloi were non-Aryan, and to be compared with the disreputable Galli of Asia Minor, *op. cit.* 101.

[3] *Il.* v. 370, 381 [ii. B]; Miss Harrison, *Prolegomena*, 317.

[4] *Il.* iii. 267 f. [ii. B]; xix. 252 f. [iv.].

[5] *Il.* ii. 755 [v.]; *Od.* x. 514; *Il.* xviii. 369 [iii. B].

which are still enforced among many savage and semi-savage races;[1] secondly, the triple offering to the dead made at the falls of Styx—mead, wine, and water—suggests chthonic rites, and has a curious analogy in the remarkable libation table found in the Dictaean Cave with its cup-like receptacles.[2] The Homeric accounts of this primitive oath-taking by Styx do not occur in what are supposed to be the earlier cantos of the *Iliad*.[3]

When we come to magic the case is similar. Thus in the case of the Aegis, Professor Ridgeway has clearly shown that the Gorgoneion on the shield is but the head of the slain beast whose skin was the raiment of the primitive goddess.[4] In the poems it appears in practically all the cantos, and is borne by Zeus, Athene, or Apollo.[5] The other magical appliances appear more often in the *Odyssey* than in the *Iliad*. In the *Iliad* we meet the magic strap or girdle of Aphrodite, which seems to have been placed in a loose fold of the robe as a mimetic charm to promote union with the beloved one.[6] It sometimes seems to stand for the Life Token, as in a Micmac story where a man captures a mermaid by obtaining the hair-string without which she could not live.[7] The magical power of the girdle seems, in other cases, to depend on the efficacy of the cord and sacred circle as a charm against evil spirits. That of Aphrodite is "broidered,

[1] *Pausanias*, iv. 253 f.

[2] *Od.* x. 519 f.; *Journal Hellenic Studies*, xvii. 358.

[3] *Il.* ii. 755 [v.], xiv. 271, xv. 37 [iii.], xxiii. 73 [iii. B]; *Od.* v. 184.

[4] *Journal Hellenic Studies*, xx. p. xliv, and see Miss Harrison, *op. cit.* 187 ff.; Elworthy (*Folk-lore*, xiv. 212 ff.) connects it in its later development with the octopus.

[5] *Il.* ii. 447, xviii. 204 (Athene) [i.], iv. 167 (Zeus) [ii. B], v. 738 (Athene), xvii. 593 (Zeus) [ii. C], xv. 229, 308, 318, 361 (Apollo) [iii.], xxiv. 20 (Apollo) [iii. B], xxi. 400 (Athene) [iv.]; *Od.* xxii. 297 (Athene).

[6] *Il.* xiv. 214 [iii.].

[7] McCulloch, *Childhood of Fiction*, 126, quoting Leland, *Algonquin Legends*, 282.

fair-wrought, wherein are all the enchantments; therein are love, and desire, and loving converse, that steals the wits even of the wise." The girdle of Hera has additional protectives in its hundred tassels, which baffle the Evil Eye, and are probably like the pendants found at Mycenae, which seem to represent a common form of amulet.[1] The Egyptian kings wore as a protective a special royal girdle, which is like the Bunna-do-At worn by the old Irish kings, and the Brahmanical cord of India.[2] Even in the Western Isles of Scotland a girdle of seal-skin is worn to cure sciatica, while one method of becoming a werwolf is to obtain a girdle made of human skin.[3] An even closer parallel to the love-girdle of Aphrodite is the magic necklace of Frey which fascinates the sons of men.[4]

The magic wand, the stock implement of all magicians and sorcerers, appears only once in the *Iliad*, but several times in the *Odyssey*.[5]

The *Iliad* provides examples of those works of art which indicate the magical qualities ascribed to the early metallurgists—the magic tripods of Hephaistos with golden wheels, which of their own motion might enter the assembly of the gods and again return to his house; the magic bellows which work at his bidding; the golden handmaids, "the semblances of living maids, who have understanding in their hearts, voice, and strength."[6] These have their analogues in the *Odyssey* in the hounds of gold and silver which guard the palace of Alcinous, and the youthful golden torch-bearers, possibly statues,[7] which may be com-

[1] *Il.* xiv. 161 [iii.]; Schuchhardt, *Schliemann's Excavations*, 180.

[2] Erman, *Life in Ancient Egypt*, 60; O'Curry, *Manners and Customs of the Ancient Irish*, iii. 174.

[3] Pinkerton, *Voyages*, iii. 595; Fiske, *Myth and Myth-makers*, 90.

[4] Thorpe, *Northern Mythology*, i. 33; Grimm, *Teutonic Mythology*, i. 307, ii. 870.

[5] *Il.* xxiv. 343 (Hermes) [iii. B]; *Od.* x. 238 (Circe), xiii. 429, xvi. 172, 456 (Athene), v. 43 ff. (Hermes).

[6] *Il.* xviii. 373, 470 [iii. B].

[7] *Od.* vii. 91, 100.

pared with the young deer, made of gold and studded with jewels, which in Somadeva's story dance in front of the maidens, and the magic figures which fan the sleepers in the palace of Ravana, or the five golden figures of men given by Kuvera, the god of wealth, to Vikramaditya, whose limbs grow again when they are cut off; and when Naravāhanadatta enters the magic city he finds all the men to be wooden figures, which moved as if they were alive, but lacked the power of speech.[1] Friar Orderic tells us that "in the palace of the Great Khan there are many peacocks of gold, and when any of the Tartars wish to amuse their lord, then they go one after another and clap their hands, upon which the peacocks clap their wings and make as if they would dance." This, he shrewdly remarks, must be done either by diabolic art or by some engine working underground; and in another place he tells of vessels of wine which lift themselves to the lips of the drinkers.[2] Such, too, were the horse of copper, the hounds, the metal serpent, which the arch-magician Virgilius made to clear Rome of evil-doers.[3] In the Teutonic legend Thor's hammer comes back of itself into his hand, like an Australian boomerang, and in the hall of Aegi the pitchers of ale brought themselves to the board, the loaves walked in, and the wine poured itself out.[4] With these magical works of art may be classed the imperishable clothing which Calypso gives to Odysseus,[5] like the invulnerable garment presented by his mother to Oddo in the Eyrbyggia Saga.[6]

In the same class are the flying sandals of Hermes, golden, divine, which bear him over the wet sea and the

[1] Tawney, *Katha*, ii. 569, i. 350, 390; Griffith, *Ramayan*, 401.

[2] Yule, *Cathay and the Way Thither*, i. 131, 143; *id. Marco Polo*,[1] i. 266, 278 ff.

[3] Hazlitt, *Tales and Legends*, 46 ff.

[4] Grimm, *Teutonic Mythology*, ii. 870.

[5] *Od.* vii. 265.

[6] Mallet, *op. cit.* 522.

boundless land with the breathings of the wind, and those of Athene which wax not old.[1] These have their analogues in the feather shift of Freyja, and the fairy shoes, the nine-leagued boots of the fairy tales, the Pushpaka or flying throne of Hindu tradition.[2] In another form we meet them in the slipper of Cinderella, and the magic shoe of the Chinese story, which the lover shakes when he wishes to summon his absent mistress.[3] In a Hindu story the hero wins them from the sons of the Asura Māya, who are represented in European tradition by the two giants in the German tale of the "Crystal Bath."[4]

It is only in the *Odyssey*[5] that we have an allusion to the treatment by the savage medicine-man, the stopping of bleeding by the recital of a charm, which appears constantly in Indian and other folk-lore. In the *Ramayana* Vrihaspati combines such spells with the use of herbs; the mere passing through the palace of the Hetaira cures the horses' wounds, as Lancelot cures the wounds of Sir Urre of Hungary; and in Celtic folk-lore the magic ointment gains its power from the spells pronounced over it.[6]

The veil, again, is used in a mystic way. In the *Odyssey* Ino Leucothea gives him the divine veil which saves Odysseus when he wraps it round his breast, the personality of the owner attaching to her clothing, as the might of Achilles is supposed to be transferred to Hector with the arms of Achilles.[7]

Circe, again, knows the magic ointment. When she anoints the swine with it, the bristles with which the

[1] *Il.* xxiv. 340 ff. [iii. B]; *Od.* v. 44 ff., i. 90 ff.

[2] Clouston, *Popular Tales*, i. 72 ff.; Grimm, *Teutonic Mythology*, i. 327, ii. 503; Tawney, *Katha*, i. 13, ii. 627; Griffith, *Ramayan*, 267.

[3] Giles, *Strange Stories*, i. 170.

[4] Tawney, *Katha*, i. 13 f.; Grimm, *Household Tales*, ii. 347.

[5] xix. 457. [Cf. *infra*, p. 89.]

[6] Griffith, *Ramayan*, 464, 482 ff.; Tawney, *Katha*, i. 348, quoting *La Mort d'Arthure*, iii. 270; Rhys, *Celtic Folk-lore*, ii. 657 n.

[7] *Od.* v. 346, 373.

venom had clothed them drop off their limbs.[1] This is like the ointment of the folk-tales, which makes him who uses it invulnerable, and restores the dead to life; if made of the fat of unbaptised babies, or of seven herbs, each picked on a special day, it gives the witch the power of riding through the air on a broomstick.[2] Another variety gives the power of seeing fairies; a third the faculty of invisibility, like the stone which Peredur receives in the Arthurian legend.[3] In the *Arabian Nights* the Merman gives Abdulla an ointment, "wherewith when thou hast anointed thy body, the water will do thee no hurt, though thou should pass the lave of thy life going about in the great deep"; and in another tale of the same collection the Fakir says: "The wonders of this ointment are passing strange and rare. An thou close thy left eye and rub upon the lid the smallest portion of the salve, then all the treasures of the world now concealed from thy gaze will come to sight"—the same ointment, in fact, which the fairies give to the human midwife who attends their wives, and which, if misused, causes blindness.[4] This and many other ideas of the same kind are survivals from the time when no one tried to draw the line between medicine and magic.

Invisibility, which in folk-lore is ordinarily secured by the use of drugs,—in Dahome by pounding up a baby boy in a mortar,—by a special stone, fernseed, and the like, is in Homer gained by a magic helmet, like that of Hades, which Athene dons that terrible Ares may not behold her. This is the Tarn-kappe of Teutonic

[1] *Od.* x. 391 ff.

[2] Hartland, *Legend of Perseus*, i. 49, 57, iii. 104; Webster, *Basque Legends*, 70.

[3] Hartland, *Science of Fairy Tales*, 59 ff.; Grimm, *Teutonic Mythology*, iii. 1210; Rhys, *Studies in the Arthurian Legend*, 87, 271.

[4] Burton, *Nights*, vii. 250, x. 175; Hartland, *Science of Fairy Tales*, 59 ff.

[5] *Il.* v. 844 ff. [iii. B]; Burton, *Mission to Gelele*, ii. 71 n.

mythology, the Dular-kufl or Hulidshjalmir of Norse legend, the cap of Perseus, the ring of Gyges, the mantle of Arthur and of the Irish Druids, and the ring of Lunid, which were reckoned among the thirteen precious things of the Island of Britain.[1] In the *Iliad*, too, the gods freely exercise the power of shedding or removing the mist which shrouds themselves or their favourites, an incident which occurs all through the epic and in the *Odyssey*.[2] So in the Irish tale, Broichan the Druid spreads a mist over St. Columba.[3]

For the witch-ointment of Circe there is a counter-charm, the "herb of virtue" which Hermes gives to Odysseus, the plant black at the root, but the flower is like to milk; the gods call it Moly, but it is hard for mortal men to dig.[4] In the word Moly some philologists see the Skr. *mūla*, "root." It is very improbable that any special plant was in the mind of the poet. The difficulty in digging it perhaps points to the mandrake, that remarkable plant with a myriad mystic virtues, which shrieks as it is drawn from the earth, and of which Pliny tells us that when they intended to take the root, "they took the wind thereof, and with a sword describing three circles round it, they digged it up looking towards the west." Josephus (*B.J.* vii. 6, 3) says that "a furrow must be drawn round the root until its lower part is exposed, then a dog is tied to it, after which the person tying the dog must get away. The dog then endeavours to follow him and so easily pulls up the root, but dies suddenly instead of his master."[5]

[1] Thorpe, *op. cit.* i. 217; Clouston, *Popular Tales*, i. 109; Lady Guest, *Mabinogion*, 286; Joyce, *Social History*, i. 245.

[2] *Il.* xv. 668; xx. 444; xxi. 597 [i.]; v. 24, 500 [ii. A]; viii. 50; xxiii. 188 [iii. B]; xi. 72 [iv.]; xvii. 269, 551 [v.]; *Od.* vi. 15; xiii. 189; xxiii. 371 f.

[3] Joyce, *Social History*, i. 223, 246.

[4] *Od.* x. 287, 302 f.

[5] Pliny, *Nat. Hist.* xxv. 94: Aubrey, *Remains of Gentilisme*, 253; Gray, *China*, i. 260; Aston, *Nihongi*, i. 208; Wilkinson, *Ancient Egyptians*, ii.

Another of these magic drugs is that which Helen learnt from Polydamnia of Egypt, that home of magic and mystery:

> "But Helen now on new device did stand,
> Infusing straight a medicine in their wine,
> That drowning care and dangers, did decline
> All thought of ill. Who drunk the cup should shed
> All that day not a tear, no, not if dead
> That day his father or his mother were,
> Nor if his brother, child, or chiefest dear
> He should see murdered there before his face."[1]

This drug of forgetfulness is a stock element in the folk-tales. In the Norse legend Grimhild gives a potion, the Ominnis-öl, to Sigfried, which makes him forget his love, Brunhild, and the same draught she gives to her daughter, Gudrun. We have the Nepenthe of Homer in the "insane herb" eaten by the companions of Sindibad, which some have tried to identify with the oriental hemp. We meet it also in the Arab tale of the "Ensorcelled Prince," and in the Hindu story Koila procures a drug from the dancing-women which causes him to forget his home, his wife, his child, as in the Irish tale the Druids give Cuchulainn the draught of oblivion.[2] In the Chinese purgatory the drink of forgetfulness is administered by an old beldame, Mother Meng. "Whether they swallow much or little it matters not; but sometimes there are perverse devils, who altogether refuse to drink. Then beneath their feet sharp blades start up, and a copper tube is put down their throats by force, by which they are compelled to swallow some."[3] The Greeks had

25, iii. 350; Miss Garnett, *Women of Turkey*, ii. 2 f.; Hastings, *Dictionary of the Bible*, iii. 234.

[1] *Od.* iv. 220 ff.

[2] *Corpus Poet. Boreale*, i. 289, 393, 395; Grimm, *Teutonic Mythology*, iii. 1101; Burton, *Nights*, i. 65; iv. 376; Wilkinson, *Ancient Egyptians*, ii. 412; Miss Frere, *Old Deccan Days*, 256; O'Curry, *Manners and Customs of the Ancient Irish*, ii. 198.

[3] Giles, *Strange Stories*, ii. 207.

the same idea in Lethe, "the place of forgetfulness" in the underworld, and the river of which when the dead drank they forgot their homes and infant children, while the modern shepherd of the islands knows of a mountain plant, "the grass of denial," of which when the sheep eat they forget their young.[1]

So far I have been dealing with some of the many folk-lore incidents which occur in the epics. From what I have said of the provenience of these incidents as illustrated by the references attached to this paper, it will, I think, be found that it is impossible to trace any stratification of these in the various cantos or lays into which some critics divide the *Iliad*. So far, this may be considered evidence in support of the view that the *Iliad* and *Odyssey* belong to a single age, if they are not the work of a single author. But this argument must not be pressed too far. The number of facts is not large enough to base a safe induction upon them. Some ideas would naturally be selected for use by the poet when dealing with special episodes in the story which he selected for treatment. Or, again, it is possible that such incidents may have become part of the stock epic machinery, and be used by one poet after another when dealing with subjects of the same class.

W. CROOKE.

(*To be continued.*)

[1] Bent, *Journal Anthropological Institute*, xv. 395; Frazer, *Pausanias*, v. 202; Miss Cox, *Cinderella*, 512 f.; Grimm, *Household Tales*, ii. 393; Ralston, *Russian Folk Tales*, 305.

SOME NOTES ON HOMERIC FOLK-LORE.

BY W. CROOKE.

(*Continued from p. 77.*)

As we have already seen, Homer carefully selects the traditions which he uses, and though he has omitted much, he has provided us with a large number of Sagas and Märchen ; the former being tales told of supernatural personages, of heroes and heroines who have definite names and are supposed to have once actually existed, or are attached to definite places ; the latter being vague, impersonal, indefinite, in short, more in the manner of the fairy tale. Some critics have attempted to draw a distinction between the two epics—that the *Iliad* is made up of Sagas, the *Odyssey* of Märchen. But this statement is not entirely accurate. Thus the main subject of the *Odyssey* is the Saga of the Absent Husband, who recovers his wife after many adventures, in which Tokens of Recognition, like the bed of Odysseus, the scar left by the boar, the facts known to Penelope and Laertes alone, form a leading part.[1] Here it may be remarked that in tales of this class the hero is very often recognised by his skill in cooking. In the *Mahabharata*, Nala is recognised in this way, and the same incident occurs in the Arab tale of Nur-al-din Ali and his son Badr-al-din Hasan, where he is identified by his skill in cooking the pomegranate conserve.[2] It is, in this light, suggestive,

[1] *Od.* xxiii. 180 ff. ; xix. 467 ff. ; xxiv. 330 ff.

[2] Burton, *Nights*, i. 224.

that when Odysseus offers to serve the Wooers he says, "No mortal may vie with me in the business of a serving-man, in piling well a fire, in cleaving dry faggots, and in carving and roasting flesh and in pouring of wine."[1] In the same category is the testing of the hero's skill in the competition of shooting through the rings of the axes, which also occurs in the Panjab tale of Rasalu, while in the *Ramayana* Rama's arrow flies through seven palm trees and through the hill behind them.[2]

Tales of the Absent Husband type are to be found in a Chinese Saga; in a Greek tale from Kato Sudena; in an Italian story; in one of Grimm's German tales; largely in ballad literature, as in those of Hind Horn and King Horn; and in the Arabian Saga of Kamar-alzaman and Badaura.[3] These tales seem to fall into two groups—one where the separation is caused by a misunderstanding; the other, where, as in the German story, the hero goes away for some other reason. With this is combined in the *Odyssey* the Saga of the Wooing and the means by which the faithful wife baffles her importunate lovers.[4]

In the Saga of Bellerophon[5] we have, first, the only

[1] *Od.* xv. 319 ff.

[2] Swynnerton, *Romantic Tales*, 213; *Cambridge Jataka*, v. 68; Griffith, *Ramayan*, 228, 338.

[3] Dennys, *Folk-lore of China*, 161; Von Hahn, *Griechische und Albanesische Märchen*, i. 266; Pitrè, *Biblioteca delle Tradizione Popolare Siciliani*, v. 146; Grimm, *Household Tales*, No. 101; Child, *English and Scottish Popular Ballads*, vol. i.; Burton, *Nights*, iii. 1 ff. For these references I am indebted to Mr. Sidney Hartland. See also Lang, *Homer and the Epic*, 226 f.

[4] This I have already discussed in *Folk-lore*, ix. 97 ff. Mr. Monro (*Odyssey*, ii. 302) objects to my solution on the ground that Telemachus claims the right to dispose of his mother's hand. This does not seem relevant. Naturally he does so as head of the house in the absence of his father. But we find that pressure is put upon her by his parents and brethren also (*Odyssey*, xv. 16, xix. 158).

[5] *Il.* vi. 155 ff. [ii. A].

mention of writing in the epics. It is remarkable that in the *Ramayana* also, the "kernel" of which was composed before 500 B.C., we have only one mention of writing in the form of marks on arrows, which were probably spells to make them reach their mark.[1] Recent enquiries show that various forms of writing were current in the eastern Aegean at a date much earlier than is commonly supposed. Cuneiform characters were probably in use in Cyprus about 1500 B.C.; the Babylonian custom of writing on clay tablets passed as far west as Crete, and it was adopted by the Mycenaeans of Knossos for their pictographic script; a system independent of this seems to have been in use in Mycenae.[2] "The clay archives of the palace of Knossos," says Mr. A. J. Evans, "conclusively show that in the Aegean world there existed, at least as early as the 15th century B.C., a highly developed form of linear script containing a series of forms practically identical with those in use down to a much later date by the Greeks of Cyprus." In the Homeric passage which we are discussing it is worth while to notice, first, that the contents of the tablet, "many deadly things" (θυμοφθόρα πολλά), seems to imply that writing was then regarded as a semi-magical art; secondly, I would venture to suggest a view which I have not seen in any of the commentaries which I have been able to consult, that the phrase describing the tablet (ἐν πίνακι πτυκτῷ), which implies, as Mr. Leaf says, a double wooden tablet with the writing inside, and sealed up, may have been an imitation of the method in use among the Babylonians of protecting valuable documents within an outer envelope of clay.[3]

[1] Griffith, *Ramayan*, 407.

[2] Hale, *The Oldest Civilisation in Greece*, 138 ff.; A. J. Evans, *Journal Hellenic Studies*, xvii. 327 ff., xxi. 339; Flinders Petrie, *Journal Anthropological Institute*, xxix. 204 f., xxx. 217.

[3] See an illustration in Maspero, *Dawn of Civilisation*, 732.

In this Saga we have also the Letter of Death, which the hero was to show to the father of Anteia that he might be slain. We are reminded of David's letter to Joab: "Set ye Uriah in the forefront of the hottest battle and retire ye from him, that he may be smitten and die"; of Somadeva's tale of Adityavarman, who directs his ally to slay the wise minister, Sivavarman, or of the treacherous queen, Kāvyā-lankārā, who plans in the same way the death of the gallant princes, the sons of her rival; of Grimm's German story of the *Devil with the Golden Hair*, where the king writes in a letter to the queen, "As soon as the boy arrives with this letter, let him be killed and buried, and all must be done before I come home"; of Ahmed the Orphan in the *Seven Wazirs*, where the bearer hands the letter to another, who suffers in his stead, whence it was adopted into the *Gesta Romanorum*, in the tale where the innocent lad delays to hear Mass, and the contriver of the plot, who bears the fatal letter, is flung into the furnace.[1] The incident, in fact, is so familiar, that in oriental folk-lore such letters have acquired a special name, "those of Mutalammis, the poet."[2]

We find, again, in the Saga of Bellerophon the very common tale of seduction successfully resisted by the continent hero, which we meet in Semitic literature in the tale of Joseph and Potiphar's wife, the Yusuf and Zuleikha of the more modern East, itself derived from the old Egyptian tale of the two brothers, Satu and Anapu.[3] Buddhist story-tellers adopted the incident in the tales of Kunāla and the wife of the Emperor

[1] II. Samuel, xi. 14; Tawney, *Katha*, i. 27, 383; *id. Kathākoça*, 172; Grimm, *Household Tales*, i. 120; Clouston, *Popular Tales*, ii. 465; *id. Sindibad*, 138; Temple-Steel, *Wideawake Stories*, 410; *North Indian Notes and Queries*, iv. 85; Knowles, *Folk Tales of Kashmir*, 48.

[2] Burton, *Nights*, xii. 68 f.

[3] Lang, *Myth, Ritual, and Religion* (ed. 1899), ii. 318 ff.; Erman, *Life in Ancient Egypt*, 378.

Asoka, Sarangdhara and his step-mother Chitrangī, Gunasarman and the wife of King Mahāsena, while the Babylonians used it in the story of Ishtar's charge against Gisdhubar.[1] In classical literature it appears in the legend of Phaedra and Hippolytus, who was worshipped as a god at Troezen, where he was regarded as a god of healing, and to him maidens before marriage offered their hair. It would be natural that the seduction myth should be connected with him to emphasise his purity.[2]

The Bellerophon Saga diverges into another cycle, that of Tasks imposed upon the hero. The king of Lycia orders him to slay Chimaira, to fight the Solymi and the Amazons. Finally, when the hero succeeds, and escapes from an ambush laid for him, he receives the hand of the king's daughter, the last an incident very common in the folk-tales and suggesting descent in the female line.[3] We find in the epics, Tasks imposed on the hero in the case of Herakles forced by Eurystheus to bring from Erebus the hound of loathed Hades, and in the story of Neleus, who would give his daughter to none save he who could drive off the kine of mighty Ephicles.[4] Of such Tasks we have many instances throughout the whole range of folk-lore. Like Herakles, Hans in the Lithuanian tale of *Strong Hand and Strong Peter* overcomes Cerberus and the Devil.[5] In a Gypsy tale from Transylvania the test is to recover a ring from a fountain of boiling water.[6] In the Eyrbyggja Saga, Styr says: "Thou shalt form a path through the

[1] Clouston, *Popular Tales*, ii. 499; Waddell, *Buddhism of Tibet*, 29; Sayce, *Hibbert Lectures*, 248; *North Indian Notes and Queries*, iv. 85; Burton, *Nights*, v. 42; Boccaccio, *Decameron*, Day ii. Novel 8.

[2] Miss Harrison, *Mythology and Monuments*, Intro. cliv.

[3] Frazer, *Lectures on Kingship*, 231 ff.

[4] *Il.* viii. 362 ff. [iii. B]; *Od.* xi. 621 ff., 288 ff., xv. 231 ff.

[5] Hartland, *Legend of Perseus*, i. 48 ff.

[6] *Ibid.* iii. 102.

rocks at Biarnarhaf, and a fence between my property and that of my neighbours; thou shalt also construct a house for the reception of my flocks, and these tasks accomplished thou shalt have Adisa to wife."[1] Homer does not mention the Task imposed upon Herakles of cleaning the Augean stable; but this is one of the three Tasks the Giant in the Highland tale of the *Battle of the Birds* requires, the others being to bring the eggs of the magpie unbroken from a lofty tree, and to thatch the byre with bird's down.[2] In another form of the story the Tasks are byre-cleaning, byre-thatching, and swan-watching.[3] So in *Nicht, Nought, Nothing* the Giant requires the boy to clean his byre, to drain a lough, and to fetch eggs from a tree.[4] In these cases, as in *Lady Featherflight*,[5] the hero is aided by the friendly daughter of the Giant, an incident which, as we shall see, appears in the Homeric tale of Proteus. The records of this cycle of tales displays infinite variety. In one of Somadeva's Hindu stories the Task is to sow an immense quantity of sesame, while in an Arabian story the lover is obliged to sift a great pile of this same grain mixed with clover seed and lentils.[6] In the Italian versions, besides the usual physical Tasks, a higher form of cultured life has suggested the winning of the bride by solving a riddle.[7]

The Chimaira, which appears in this Homeric Saga—"the unconquerable one," "of divine birth was she and not of men, in front a lion and behind a serpent, and

[1] Mallet, *Northern Antiquities*, 526.

[2] Campbell, *Popular Tales of Western Highlands*, i. 29 ff.

[3] MacInnes-Nutt, *Waifs and Strays of Celtic Tradition*, 436 f.

[4] Lang, *Custom and Myth*, 90.

[5] *Folk-lore Congress Report*, 40 ff.

[6] Tawney, *Katha*, i. 360; Burton, *Nights*, xi. 159.

[7] Crane, *Italian Popular Tales*, 66 f.; Max Müller, *Contributions to the Science of Mythology*, i. 80 ff. For Tasks generally, McCulloch, *Childhood of Fiction*, 17, 392.

she breathed out dread fierceness of blazing fire," in another place called "the bane of many a man"[1]—is the only Homeric example of the fell beasts of later Greek and oriental mythology. Such were the fantastic monsters of Egypt and Babylonia.[2] By some she has been less probably identified with a volcano, and Pliny[3] tells of a Lycian mountain of that name which poured forth fire continually. But she seems rather akin to the tribe of monsters, like the later Harpies, Cerberus, the Hydra of Lerna, and the Sphinx.

This leads us to the Centaurs. Homer does not mention the horse Centaurs, which were a creation of later writers; and Ixion, their reputed father, is not named in the epics, where he might have been classed with those famous criminals, Sisyphus and Tantalus, who expiate their crimes in the underworld. Homer seems to regard the Centaurs as men. He speaks of the famous heroes who destroyed the Pheres, or wild men of the mountain caves; he tells how the renowned Centaur, Eurytion, went to the Lapithae, and how when his soul was darkened with wine he wrought foul deeds in the house of Peirithous, how the heroes mutilated him with the sword, and ever after with darkened mind he bare about with him the burden of his sins in the foolishness of his heart.[4] Hence arose the feud between the Centaurs and the sons of men. Of this remarkable myth many explanations have been suggested. Some have supposed that it describes the contest between civilised man and the aborigines; others see in it a comparison of the mountain torrents with galloping horses. To one school of mythologists, now in disrepute, it was sufficient to derive the name from the Gandharva

[1] *Il.* vi. 179 ff. [ii. A], xvi. 325 ff. [i.].

[2] Maspero, *Dawn of Civilisation*, 84, 539, 582; Renouf, *Hibbert Lectures*, Intro. 20; Sayce, *Ibid.* 392.

[3] *Nat. Hist.* ii. 106, v. 28.

[4] *Il.* i. 266 ff. [i.], ii. 742 [iv.].

singers of Hindu myth, though Cheiron alone is said to have been skilled in music. This derivation is now generally abandoned.[1] The connexion, again, of the Centaurs with Thessaly has been supposed to imply horse worship, while others suggest an ass cult.[2] Recently a more plausible explanation has been suggested by Professor Gardner, that they are forest or mountain spirits, a common folk belief representing that the devastation caused by hurricanes is due to the conflict of these spirits when they hurl tree-trunks and rocks at each other. "The appropriateness of the form of the horse, or of association with the horse, to spirits that ride the storm, is both obvious in itself and attested by numerous instances from folk-lore; but the peculiar form taken by this association in the earliest Greek Centaurs, which are merely men with a horse's body and hind quarters growing out of their back, is probably due to some accidental association, or to some too literal interpretation of a metaphor used by an early poet."[3]

Next comes the tale of the Amazons. Professor Geddes remarks that they appear only in what he calls the Ulyssean cantos of the *Iliad*, where he finds frequent indications of oriental influence.[4] Priam says that he was an ally of the men of Phrygia when the Amazons came, and the third task imposed on the Lycian Bellerophon was to slay the Amazons, women peers of men. According to one theory, the legend of these warrior women is based on the hosts of female slaves employed in the temples of Asia Minor and the further east.[5] But against this it may be urged that the legend

[1] Macdonell, *Vedic Mythology*, 137.

[2] Geddes, *Problem of the Homeric Poems*, 246 f.; *Journal Hellenic Studies*, xiv. 90.

[3] *Journal Hellenic Studies*, xvii. 301.

[4] *Problem*, 284 f.; *Il.* iii. 189 [ii. B], vi. 186 [ii. A].

[5] Sayce, *Hibbert Lectures*, 235; Müller, *Dorians*, E.T. i. 405.

has a much wider provenance, and the stories of the many kingdoms in which women by the law of succession and otherwise asserted superiority over men may be connected with the matriarchate or with crude ideas of conception, such as those adopted by the Australian Arunta.[1] Stories of this kind are current in South America, which are supposed to be based either on the warlike character of the women of some tribes or on the effeminate appearance of the men.[2] In the east we meet many stories of a Kingdom of Women, such as that of Rāma Paramita in the *Mahabharata,* which also appears in Chinese tradition, and in the "Island of Wāk" and the "City of Women" in the *Arabian Nights.*[3] Among a people beyond Cathay the women were said to have reason like men, while the males were great hairy dogs; even nowadays in Assam there is a tale of a village in which only women dwell; near Sumatra is an island of women, who, like the mares in Virgil's *Georgics,* conceive by the agency of the wind.[4] The same legend appears in North Europe, where in the Celtic land of the Everliving "there is no race but women and maidens alone."[5] It is current among the Ainos of Japan; in Africa it is supported by accounts of the female bodyguard of the kings of Dahome and Ashanti; and North American tradition tells of an island in which the men are ruled by a tall, fair woman.[6] The story is, in short,

[1] Spencer-Gillen, *Tribes of Central Australia,* 663.

[2] Bates, *A Naturalist on the River Amazon,* i. 215 n.; Frazer, *Pausanias,* ii. 139.

[3] Yule, *Marco Polo,*[1] ii. 396; Burton, *Nights,* vi. 217, vii. 252.

[4] Yule, *Cathay and the Way Thither,* i. Intro. 129; Gait, *Assam Census Report,* 1891, i. 250; Marsden, *History of Sumatra,* 297.

[5] Rhys, *Celtic Folk-lore,* ii. 661; Borlase, *Dolmens of Ireland,* iii. 777; Pinkerton, *Voyages,* iii. 704.

[6] Chamberlain, *Aino Folk Tales,* 37; Bancroft, *Native Races of the Pacific States,* iii. 153; Burton, *Mission to Galele,* ii. 63; Im Thurn, *Among the Indians of Guiana,* 385.

a world-wide myth which was adopted by Greek story-tellers.

Another tale of the same kind reported by early mariners appears in Homer's account of the Cranes, who with approaching winter wing their flight to the streams of Ocean, bearing slaughter and fate to the Pygmy race.[1] The orderly flight of the cranes in the direction of the great African lakes naturally gave rise to the belief that they marched as an army does to attack an enemy, and this enemy could only be the Pygmies, whom recent explorations have made familiar to us. Accounts of them must at an early date have reached the Greeks through the Egyptians, to whom they were familiar.[2] Such travellers' tales did not lose in the telling, and the story was more generally believed in Europe as these Pygmies came to be connected with the tiny fairies which occupy the burial mounds. The course of the myth was perhaps from west to east; and so they come into the tale of *Sindibad the Seaman*, and even the matter-of-fact traveller, Marco Polo, identified them with the apes of Java.[3]

Iphimedeia, wife of Aloeus, bore, we are told, twin sons to Poseidon, Otos and Ephialtes. Doomed to enjoy but short life, they were far the tallest men that earth ever reared, and the goodliest after Orion. At nine years of age they were in breadth nine cubits and nine fathoms high. They threatened war on the gods, and essayed to pile Ossa on Olympus, and on Ossa Pelion, that there might be a pathway to the sky; and this they would have accomplished had they reached full manhood. But Apollo slew them ere their cheeks were

[1] *Il.* iii. 2 ff. [ii. A].

[2] Maspero, *Dawn of Civilisation*, 397, 428.

[3] Tylor, *Primitive Culture*,[2] i. 388; Burton, *Nights*, iv. 364; Yule, *Marco Polo*,[1] ii. 228; Pinkerton, *Voyages*, iii. 601; Sir T. Brown, *Works*, i. 424; Yule, *Cathay and the Way Thither*, i. 122.

darkened with the bloom of youth.[1] In another passage we learn that they tried to bind Ares, a legend which I have elsewhere discussed.[2] They are by affiliation akin to the Moliones and Polyphemus,[3] a fact which indicates that some attempt was made to include them in the Olympian dynasty, the story of the descent from rivers being here replaced by the fatherhood of Poseidon; the same transition shows itself in the curious tale of Tyro, whom Poseidon wooes in the form of Enipeus, the river god.[4] Secondly, like so many Homeric demigods, they appear in pairs, like Podaleirios and Machaon, Peisandros and Hippolochos, Lykaon and Polydoros, Kreithon and Orsilochos. The same idea appears in the twin groups of Achilles-Patroclus, Theseus-Peirithoos, Phaethon-Helios, Pelias-Neleus, Prometheus-Epimetheus, Odysseus-Telemachus, Eteokles-Polyneikes, and the Dioscuri. In Rome we have Romulus-Remus; in India the two Asvins, Rama-Lakshmana, Krishna-Balarāma, Yama-Yamī, Yajna-Dakshina, Pūshan-Indra. Similarly related are the Norse Odinn-Loki, the Egyptian Osiris-Set, the Huron Ioskeha-Tawis, the Persian Ormuzd-Ahriman. In these pairs of male gods their association possibly points either to the syncretism of allied cults, or to the development of new cults out of a primitive cult epithet; where the pair are male and female it suggests the union of the male and female principles.

Thirdly, in this legend we have the familiar tale of the attempt to scale the heavens. In the Hindu version the Asuras build a fire-altar in the hope of reaching the sky. Each of them placed a brick on it, and Indra, passing himself off as a Brahman, added one for himself. At last Indra pulled out his brick, and the Asuras fell down and were turned into spiders, except two of them, who flew away to heaven and became the heavenly

[1] *Od.* xi. 305 ff.

[2] *Folk-lore*, viii. 325 ff.

[3] *Il.* xi. 750 ff. [iv.]; *Od.* ix. 412.

[4] *Od.* xi. 235 ff.

dogs. The bricks here may be compared to the mountains in the Greek myth.[1] So the Egyptian story tells of an ascent to heaven by a tower, the Babel of Semitic tradition, or the attempt of Nimrod to climb to the sky.[2] In the common European version we have *Jack and the Beanstalk*, where the boy climbs to the sky and robs the Giant of his treasures, a tale of the class in which the culture-hero, like Prometheus, steals something necessary to mankind from the people of the other world. The motif has been moralised in the remarkable Indian tale of *Sedit and the Two Brothers Hus*, in which the brothers abandon the attempt on the ground that theirs is a mistaken ideal, and that it is better for men to live and work on earth rather than enjoy the passive repose of heaven.[3]

Fourthly, we have the tale of the *Precocious Children*. In the Homeric Hymn, Apollo new-born tastes the nectar and ambrosia, leaps from his swaddling-clothes, begins to speak, and wanders through the land. In the Norse tale, Vali, when one night old, sallies forth to avenge the death of Balder; and Magni, when three years old, flings the enormous foot of the Giant Hrungnir off his father, and would have beaten the monster to death with his fists.[4] The Hindus tell equally marvellous tales of the might of the infant Krishna, and the Dayaks have a divine child in Seragunting.[5] Robert the Devil bites off the paps of his nurse, is fed through a horn, and surpasses in strength and wisdom all the children of his age; and Tom Hickathrift, "at ten years old, was six feet high and three feet across, with a hand like a shoulder of mutton, and everything else pro-

[1] *Sacred Books of the East*, xii. 286, xlii. 500.

[2] Maspero, *Life in Egypt*, 212; Sale, *Koran*, 269 n. 1. For the Malay version, Skeat-Blagden, *Pagan Races*, ii. 300.

[3] *Folk-lore*, x. 344 ff.

[4] Grimm, *Teutonic Mythology*, i. 320 f.

[5] Roth, *Natives of Sarawak*, i. 198 f.

portionable."[1] As St. Benedict sang Eucharistic hymns before he was born, so the Zulu tale tells of a child who sings in his mother's womb, and the modern Lamas of Tibet are said when only a few months old to have full powers of speech.[2]

In the famous tale of Niobe and her children we reach the cycle of myths based on the common belief in the petrifaction of human beings, some accidental conformation of mountain, rock, or tree being accepted as the basis of the story. Of Niobe Homer tells us that Apollo slew her sons and Artemis her daughters, for that she matched herself with Leto, saying that the goddess bare only twain, but herself many children. Nine days they lay in their blood and there was none to bury them, for Kronion turned the folk to stone. But at last the gods buried them:

> "Haply she now, a rock amongst the rocks,
> Amid the desert hills of Sipylus,
> There where they say the Nymphs divine, who whirl
> In dance round Acheloius, make their couch,
> Changed though she be to stone, retains her woe."[3]

This famous rock of Niobe Pausanias tells us he saw himself, and from his account it was undoubtedly a rock, not an image of Cybele, with which attempts have been made to identify it.[4] It is needless to illustrate this legend by parallels. But it may be noted that Homer has other cases of petrifaction, all probably based on the same idea. Thus the mixing bowls, jars of stone, and stone looms of the Nymphs, which Odysseus saw in the Cave of the Naiads, were probably some form of stalactite, as in Ireland a group of dolmens

[1] Hazlitt, *Tales and Legends*, 59, 431.

[2] Callaway, *Nursery Tales*, i. 6; Waddell, *Buddhism of Tibet*, 247.

[3] *Il.* xxiv. 602 ff. [iii. B].

[4] *Pausanias*, i. 21, 3; ii. 21, 9, 13, 7, with Frazer's notes; *Journal Hellenic Studies*, i. 88, iii. 39 ff., 61 ff.

is supposed to consist of petrified weavers' spools.[1] The ship of the Phaeacians which Poseidon smote into stone is probably represented by the rock Karavi off the harbour of Corcyra, if M. Bérard's identification of this and the Cave of the Cyclops with the Cave of Sejanus at Cumae, where two great obelisks represent the rocks flung by the monster, be accepted. In another passage the son of crooked-counselling Kronos turns the snake into stone.[2]

The legend of Proteus embodies several familiar incidents. In the *Odyssey* Proteus is fixed, perhaps by Cretan sailors, at the mouth of the Nile, in Egypt.[3] Pausanias describes the worship of "The Old Man of the Sea" at Gythium, and this is the title by which he is known in the *Iliad*, where, however, no local habitation is assigned to him.[4] Homer says that he knows the depths of every sea and that he is thrall of Poseidon. His later representations suggest his connexion with a fish-god, like that of Nineveh, and Mr. Hall with some hesitation compares him to Dagon.[5] In any case, he appears to be a disestablished sea-god, and in the later accounts, as in that of Diodorus and Herodotus,[6] he seems to have oriental affinities. Proteus, Homer tells us, sleeps with his flock of seals in a hollow cave; he can change himself into the shapes of all manner of things that creep upon the earth, into water and burning fire. When Odysseus seizes him he becomes successively a lion, a snake, a pard, a boar, running water, a tall and flowering tree.[7] This power of transformation is common in the folk-tales. In Norse tradition, for instance, the Trollman and the witch could appear as whales or

[1] *Od.* xiii. 105 f.; Borlase, *Dolmens of Ireland*, iii. 769.
[2] *Il.* ii. 319 [ii. A].
[3] *Od.* iv. 365, 385.
[4] *Il.* xviii. 140 f. [iii. B], *Pausanias*, iii. 21, 9, with Frazer's note.
[5] Layard, *Nineveh*, ii. 466 f.; Hall, *Oldest Civilisation*, 135 n.
[6] *Diod.* i. 62; *Herod.* ii. 112.
[7] *Od.* iv. 384 ff.

other animals, and the Trollwife, in order to kill King Frodi, transforms herself into a sea cow and her sons into calves.[1] In another tale Hardgrip says to Hadding: "Be not moved by my unwonted look of size. For my substance is sometimes thinner, sometimes ampler; now meagre, now abundant; and I alter and change at my pleasure the condition of my body, which is at one time shrivelled up, and at another expanded; now my tallness reaches to the heavens, and now I settle down into a human being, under a more bounded shape."[2] In his reluctance to prophesy Proteus is like other sea gods. The taciturn, prophetic Marmennil of Germany is fished out of the sea and requires to be allowed to dive again into the depths, and the Chaldaean Eabani, who pastures the flocks of the sea, must be seized by wiles.[3]

But it is the Transformation Combat which is most prominent in the tale of Proteus. One of the best examples of this incident is the terrible scene in the tale of the "Second Calendar" in the *Arabian Nights*, where oriental fancy reaches the highest pitch of tragedy, as the Ifrit becomes successively a lion, a scorpion, a wolf, and a cock, and finally blazing fire which consumes the unlucky princess.[4] In a Hindu tale Somada becomes a black mare, and Bandhumochanī, as a bay mare, overcomes her; in the Norwegian tale of *Farmer Weathersky* the youth turns into a horse and is sold, and when the farmer seizes the ring of the princess it slips into the ashes, and he becomes a cock which begins to scratch in the ashes in search of the ring, whereupon the boy changes into a fox and bites off the cock's head.[5] In a modern Greek story, when

[1] Thorpe, *Northern Mythology*, i. 216. [2] *Saxo*, i. 21.

[3] Grimm, *Teutonic Mythology*, i. 434; Maspero, *Dawn of Civilisation*, 576 n.

[4] Burton, *Nights*, i. 123 ff.

[5] Tawney, *Katha*, i. 342 f.; Hartland, *Legend of Perseus*, ii. 56 f.; Dasent, *Popular Tales*, 335 f.; Clouston, *Popular Tales*, i. 482 ff.

the musician catches the Nereid, she becomes a dog, a serpent, a camel, and fire; but he holds on to her till the cocks begin to crow, when she resumes her original form, follows him quietly, and becomes his wife.[1] In a German tale of the same cycle the magician finds the youth reading one of his magical books, and when he tries to seize him the boy turns into a bird of prey and flies away. Finally, the magician becomes a grain of corn, which the boy in the form of a cock promptly eats, and thus the career of the warlock ends.[2] The combat, again, often takes the form of a struggle by the Giant to pass his soul into something else, in the course of which he attempts to gain his purpose by a series of magical transformations, as in the Highland tales of the *Young King of Easaidh* or *The Fair Gruagach*.[3]

This cycle would naturally connect itself with Proteus, if we accept the theory that he is a seal-god, because this animal, in virtue of its semi-human appearance, is supposed to be specially capable of transformation. "In the Faroe Islands," says Thorpe,[4] "the superstition is current that the seal every ninth night assumes a human form and dances and amuses itself like a human being, until it resumes its skin and again becomes a seal. It once happened that a man passing by during one of these transformations, and seeing the skin, took possession of it, when the seal, which was a female, not finding her skin to creep into, was obliged to continue in human form, and being a comely person the man made her his wife, had several children by her, and they lived happily together, until after a lapse of several years she chanced to find her skin, which she could not refrain from creeping into, and so became a seal again." The tale thus diverges into the Swan Maiden cycle, which is

[1] Frazer, *Pausanias*, iii. 614. [2] Grimm, *Household Tales*, i. 431.

[3] Campbell, *Popular Tales*, i. 21, ii. 437.

[4] *Northern Mythology*, ii. 173.

often in Celtic tradition connected with the seal.[1] In Germany the seal is supposed to possess the same power of shape-changing; in the Hebrides sailors suppose that drowned people turn into seals; the South American Indians believe that porpoises are water women, and the sea-cows of South African rivers are identified with the mermaids.[2]

The last incident of the Proteus tale to which I shall refer concerns Eidothee, his daughter, who instructs Odysseus how he may snare her father. In many of the tales of the Outwitted Giant cycle it is his wife, mother, or daughter who has pity on the stranger and points out a way for his escape. Thus in the German tale of *The Devil and the Three Golden Hairs* it is the Devil's grandmother who saves the stranger; in one version of *The Iron Stove* the cannibal's wife saves the maiden; in the Italian tale *Thirteenth* the ogress protects the boy from her husband; and it would have gone hard with Jack when he climbed the Beanstalk if the kindly giantess had not protected him, as in the Basque tale of *Errua the Madman*, the old woman explains to the hero how he may evade the Tartaro.[3]

The myth of the Sirens, as told in the *Odyssey*,[4] describes them as a pair of maidens who sit in a meadow and entice wayfarers by their singing. Round them lies a great pile of the bones of men, corrupt in death, and about the bones the skin is wasting. Odysseus escapes from them by anointing the ears of his comrades

[1] Kennedy, *Legendary Fictions*, 109; Curtin, *Tales of the Faeries*, 150 ff.

[2] Pinkerton, *Voyages*, iii. 595, 699, 788; Grimm, *Teutonic Mythology*, iii. 1095 n.; Crantz, *History of Greenland*, i. 339 ff.; O'Grady, *Silva Gadelica*, 72; Im Thurn, *Among Indians*, 40; Rogers, *Social Life in Scotland*, iii. 219; Reade, *Savage Africa*, 467.

[3] Grimm, *Household Tales*, i. 122, ii. 426, 564; Crane, *Italian Folk Tales*, 90 f.; Webster, *Basque Legends*, 6 ff.

[4] *Od.* xii. 39 ff., 166 ff.

with wax, and compelling them to bind him to the ship-mast. Many interpretations of this myth have been suggested—that their songs are the sighing of the wind in the trees, like the music of Orpheus or the flute of the Pied Piper, which neither beast nor man can resist; that their music is the murmur of the waves amid the hollow caves and over broken rocks; that they represent the belt of calms so dreaded by seamen; that they are the witches of the dangerous shoal water. An archaic cult statue of Hera Coronea, described by Pausanias, shows her holding the Sirens in her hand, on which Mr. Farnell remarks that "the Sirens are most commonly sepulchral symbols, emblems of the lower world, and called 'daughters of the earth' by Euripides; and if Hera were an earth-goddess, the Sirens would be naturally explained. But they were also regarded as the personifications of charm and attractiveness, and on the hand of Hera they may simply denote the fascinations of married life."[1]

These witch-maidens abound in other mythologies. They are the bird-maidens or Gandharvīs of Buddhist tales, who charm travellers by their singing;[2] the Rākshasīs or ogresses of India, who live on human flesh, and change themselves into lovely maidens who seduce voyagers. These steel themselves against their charms when they find the mangled remains of former victims. Closer still is the analogy of the Slavonic tale, where the three sisters set out in search of the Water of Life, and enter the garden where the trees sing so sweetly that every one stops to listen, and is forthwith turned, like Niobe, into stone; but the youngest sister, as is usual in myth, escapes by closing her ears with dough and wax, and thus passes through the enchanted garden in safety.[3] In an Irish tale the Druids advise

[1] *Pausanias*, ix. 34, 3; Farnell, *Cults*, i. 184.

[2] *Indian Antiquary*, x. 291 f.

[3] Frazer, *Pausanias*, v. 171.

the travellers to close their ears with wax to avoid the fascinations of the mermaids.[1]

We have, again, the water witches who annually demand a human victim, like the spirit of the Fulda and Necker in Germany, the Lorelei of the Rhine, the Drome in Normandy, Peg Powler, Nanny Powler, Peg O'Nell and Jenny Greenteeth of North England, or the Kelpie and its kinsfolk in Scotland.[2] "The river Dart every year claims its heart" is a South of England saying. Akin to these are the Nixen of Germany, the Huldra which sings in the mountains, and the Grim which lives by waterfalls and entices travellers by her music.[3] The Norwegian mermaid lulls mariners to sleep by her songs, as do the Morrows of Ireland and the Nixen of the Netherlands, who come out of rivers and sing with magical sweetness.[4] In one of the Scotch ballads a mermaid decoys a knight to his doom, and the same tale is told of Slavonian water sprites.[5] In short, dancing, song, and music are the delight of these fairy denizens of the water. Of the Rākshasīs of Ceylon the old Buddhist traveller tells that, like the Sirens, they receive travellers with flowers, scents, and music, the meadow in which they dwell being specially described, as in some of the Irish versions of the tale; finally, they shut up their visitors in an iron prison and devour them.[6] So the Pragangan of Java live on the banks of streams and madden men with their singing.[7] As in the case of the Sirens, the power of prophecy, the interpretation of dreams, and other uncanny arts are attributed

[1] O'Curry, *Manners and Customs of the Ancient Irish*, iii. 384.

[2] Hartland, *Legend of Perseus*, iii. 81 ff.; Henderson, *Folk-lore of the Northern Counties*, 265 f.; *Denham Tracts*, ii. 42.

[3] Thorpe, *Northern Mythology*, i. 246, ii. 3, 23.

[4] *Ibid.* ii. 27, iii. 199.

[5] *Folk-lore Record*, ii. 105, iv. 62 ff.

[6] Beal, *Si-yu-ki*, ii. 240 ff.; Tawney, *Katha*, ii. 638.

[7] Featherman, *Papuo-Melanesians*, 396.

to water or wood sprites, like the Latin Fauni, who controlled the rustic oracles.[1]

Homer evidently recognises something uncanny about the Sirens, because, contrary to his usual practice, he says nothing about their parentage or origin. Hence there is much to be said for Miss Harrison's theory that they were originally a form of the Keres or death sprites, and that Homer "by the magic of his song lifted them once for all out of the region of mere bogeydom."[2] Accordingly, in later Greek art they are represented as winged sprites on tombs, probably originally placed there as a sort of charm to guard the dead from evil spirits, and afterwards regarded as tender mourners lamenting the untimely fate of youth or maiden snatched away in their bloom. Their successors are the angels on our sepulchral monuments, who waft the weary spirit to its rest.

In the story of Polyphemus, the Cyclops, we reach the cycle of the Baffled Giant. This famous myth would need a paper to itself; but as it has been considered by Lauer, Grimm, and Mr. McCulloch,[3] I shall note only a few points in the story. In the first place, it looks as if the Cyclops was really a disestablished or semi-forgotten deity. Pausanias, speaking of Corinth, says: "There is also an ancient sanctuary called the altar of the Cyclopes; and they sacrifice to the Cyclopes on it."[4] He tells us nothing more, and even the learning of Dr. Frazer has been unable to unearth any further account of this cult. The name of the Cyclops, Polyphemus, "the much sayer," has been compared with that of the Celtic Gwyd Gwydion, "son of saying," in allusion to his powers of soothsaying or vaticination.[5] He alone of the Cyclopes is called one-

[1] Rhys, *Hibbert Lectures*, 198.

[2] *Prolegomena*, 197 ff.; *Myths and Monuments*, 582 ff.

[3] See Merry-Riddell, *Odyssey*, i. 546 ff.; McCulloch, *Childhood of Fiction*, 279 ff.; Frazer, *Pausanias*, v. 343 ff.

[4] *Pausanias*, ii. 2, 2.

[5] Rhys, *Hibbert Lectures*, 280 f.

eyed, a characteristic he shares with the smith-god of Japan,[1] and a host of other monsters—the Irish giant Balor, who had one eye in his forehead and another at the back of his skull, the former being never opened except on the field of battle, when it always took four men with hooks to raise the lid, and then his glance enfeebled a whole army of his enemies; the same tale is told of the monsters Kabandha and Vaisravana in the *Ramayana*.[2] In a tale from Syra the monster is half man, with only one eye, one hand, and one foot; Celtic legend tells of the Angling Giant, who had only one eye, and the ocean rose no higher than his knee; in the Irish tale of Diarmaid and Grainne, as in the Arthurian story of Peridun, the giant, like the Basque Tartaro, has only one eye in the centre of his forehead.[3]

The blinding of the monster with a red-hot poker need not detain us. It is thus that Popelusa, the Hungarian Cinderella, dealt with the one-eyed giant; the Basque hero with the Tartaro; and Bissat blinds the Tartar monster Depeghoz.[4] It is perhaps a reminiscence of the Homeric story that Sindibad in his Third Voyage, Oscar in the Highland, and Lug in the Celtic story in the same way deal with their monsters.[5]

As to the escape under the belly of the ram—in one of the Russian tales, the blacksmith who is enslaved by the witch puts on his pelisse inside-out, feigns himself to be a sheep, and passes out with the rest of the flock, as in one of the Highland variants the hero escapes by flaying

[1] Aston, *Nihongi*, i. 81 n.

[2] O'Donovan, *Four Masters*, i. 18; Joyce, *Social History*, i. 309; Hartland, *Legend of Perseus*, i. 15; Griffith, *Ramayan*, 311.

[3] MacInnes-Nutt, *Waifs and Strays*, 263; *Folk-lore*, vii. 223; Rhys, *Studies in the Arthurian Legend*, 92; *id. Hibbert Lectures*, 314; Borlase, *Dolmens of Ireland*, iii. 888; Webster, *Basque Legends*, 5.

[4] Miss Cox, *Cinderella*, 208, 489; Grimm, *Teutonic Mythology*, ii. 554; Webster, *Basque Legends*, 5.

[5] Burton, *Nights*, iv. 367; Campbell, *Popular Tales*, iii. 314; Rhys, *Hibbert Lectures*, 317.

the Giant's dog and puts on its skin; the escape under the sheep's belly in the Basque version seems to be obviously a reminiscence of Homer's story.[1] In the Celtic *Voyage of Maildune* we have another account of a similar escape. The adventurers approach an island inhabited by gigantic blacksmiths, and one burly fellow rushes out with a piece of glowing iron in the tongs, and flings it after the curragh, which, however, it fortunately misses.[2] A similar tale is also told of St. Brendan. In some cases, as in the remarkable parallel from Yorkshire, in which Jack blinds the Giant, skins his dog, and throwing the hide over his shoulder runs out on all fours barking between the legs of the monster, it has been suggested that the tradition is independent of the *Odyssey*.[3] Others see in this and the very similar tale of Conall Cra Buidhe from Islay distinct evidence of borrowing from the Homeric original.[4] It is more probable that the Cyclops Saga is made of very ancient folk-tradition, and that later versions were shaped by the splendid imaginativeness of Homer's story.

The device by which Odysseus calls himself Outis or "Nobody" appears in the Highland tale of the Brollichan who is scalded by the woman. She gives her name as "Myself," and the goblin, when asked who scalded him, answers "Myself," the same idea forming the motif of the English story *My own Self* and the Basque *Fairy in the House*.[5]

[1] Gubernatis, *Zoological Mythology*, i. 408 n.; *Folk-lore Congress Report*, 325; Webster, *Basque Legends*, 5.

[2] Joyce, *Social History*, ii. 304.

[3] Henderson, *Folk-lore of the N. Counties*, 195.

[4] Campbell, *Popular Tales*, i. 105 ff.; Jacobs, *More English Fairy Tales*, 228; *id. Celtic Fairy Tales*, 247.

[5] Campbell, *Popular Tales*, i. Intro. 47; Jacobs, *More English Fairy Tales*, 221; Webster, *Basque Legends*, 55; Clouston, *Book of Noodles*, 194; cf. Cox, *Mythology of the Aryan Nations*, ii. 366; Burton, *Nights*, xi. 31; *Folk-lore*, vii. 154 f.

The second cannibal-tale in the *Odyssey* is that of the Laestrygons.[1] Various theories have been suggested as to the position of this people. On the one hand it has been argued that the scene of the legend lies in Sicily, and that the curious statement of the poet—"where herdsman hails herdsman as he drives in his flock, and the other who drives forth answers the call; there might a sleepless man have earned a double wage, the one as neatherd, the other shepherding white flocks; so near are the outgoings of the night and day"—refers to the danger from gadflies which prevents the cattle from pasturing except after sundown, while the sheep, protected by their fleeces, could feed during the day. The reference to the smoke rising from the land[2] might, it has been thought, be based on an eruption of Etna. This view has been rightly rejected.[3] Another solution has been proposed by Dr. Verrall. "It seems more probable that 'Fargate of the Laestrygons' is, or originally was, a picture coloured, if not drawn, from the report of some terrified mariners, who, trading from lands of pasture and agriculture, saw for the first time some place, on the Euxine, maybe, where metal-work was practised on a large scale; a sort of Black Country, where 'the smoke went up from the land,' where the trolly, on paths of incredible facility, rolled down from the hills the wood for the furnaces, where shifts so extended the hours of labour that 'night and day met in one,' and where the visitor, roughly handled by the hard workmen and appalled by the signs of their skill and power, fled away to report that their figures were gigantic, and that they lived, like the Martians of Mr. Wells' romance, on the flesh of men."[4] He suggests that there is nothing inconsistent in this view with the possibility of a reference to the short summers of the

[1] *Od.* x. 50 ff. [2] *Od.* x. 99. [3] Merry-Riddell, *Odyssey*, x. 81.

[4] *Journal Hellenic Studies*, xviii. 7 f.

North, of which a rumour would first reach the Greeks on the Euxine.

All the probabilities, however, point to the North as the scene of the story. The short nights and the volcanic outbursts suit the North of Europe, of which Homer seems to have gained some knowledge, if the island of Aeolus represents an iceberg, and if the Phaeacian legend was suggested by the Northern tale of the Ferrymen of the Dead. His account of the land of the Cimmerians seems to support this inference.[1] The communication between North Europe and the Mediterranean along the Amber Route must date from a very early period, and this traffic continued during the Bronze Age.[2]

It must be remembered that there are traditions of cannibalism in North Europe in early times, and some evidence in support of the belief that it prevailed there.[3] As a proof of this the condition of the bones found in the barrows has been adduced; but, as Dr. Windle remarks, this conclusion is not quite certain.[4] St. Jerome, whatever his evidence may be worth, testifies to cannibalism among the Celts, and the folk-lore tradition is abundant, as in the case of the Celtic fairies, the Russian Baba Yaga, the hags or ogresses of the Eskimo tribes, and even some versions of our own *Blue Beard* cycle,[5] which would have been sufficient to suggest the idea to the Homeric Greeks.

Of the Lotos-eaters we are told that whoever ate the honey-sweet fruit of the lotos had no more wish to bring tidings or to come back, but rather chose to abide with the lotos-eating men, ever feeding on the lotos and for-

[1] *Od.* xi. 14 ff.

[2] Ridgeway, *Folk-lore*, i. 82 ff.; Montelius, *Journal Anthropological Institute*, xxx. 89 ff.

[3] Borlase, *Dolmens of Ireland*, ii. 469. On the cannibalism of the Celtic fairies, see Rhys, *Celtic Folklore*, ii. 673.

[4] *Remains of the Prehistoric Age*, 138.

[5] McCulloch, *Childhood of Fiction*, 289 ff.

getful of his return.[1] What the plant may have been to which Homer refers need not concern us here, for the Potion of Forgetfulness appears in the traditions of many races. One special form of it is the belief that those who eat the food of spirit-land, as in the case of Persephone and Kore, never return. A Maori tale ascribes much the same effect to the sweet potato, as the Sioux story does to the rice of the other world.[2] In the Norse legend, when Gorm went to the realm of Guthmundas, the king offered him his daughter in marriage. He was prescient enough to decline, but four of his men could not resist the temptation, and paid the penalty with loss of memory and enfeebled minds;[3] a situation reproduced with admirable power in Kingsley's *Westward Ho!* So Gudmund saps the chastity of the Danes: "The infection maddened them, distraught their wits, and blotted out their recollection." Thorkill, like Odysseus, tries to save his comrades, and gives them a horn smeared with fat as an antidote to the fascination.[4] With this we may compare the common belief in the miraculous lapse of time in fairyland.

Thus the tale of the Lotos-eaters is linked with the witcheries of Circe and Calypso. The one is usually taken to be a double of the other. In many respects the situation is the same; but there is one important difference. Calypso lives in a cave, Circe in a palace, the latter representing the fascination of a life of refined luxury, as contrasted with semi-savagery. Both are fair and lovely goddesses, dwelling in a remote isle, and attended by handmaidens; both are connected with gold and silver, and weave a mighty web as they sing; both are fair-haired awful goddesses of mortal speech; the

[1] *Od.* ix. 82 ff.

[2] Tylor, *Primitive Culture*,[2] ii. 51 ff.

[3] Rydberg, *Teutonic Mythology*, 213.

[4] Elton-Powell, *Saxo*, 346 ff.; cf. Thorpe, *Northern Mythology*, i. 103, 216, ii. 91; Rhys, *Celtic Folk-lore*, i. 113.

abode of both is surrounded by woods; both love the hero, who unwillingly responds to their passion; neither of them is permitted to retain him for ever; each solemnly swears not to injure him; each at dawn arrays herself in a great shining robe, light of woof and gracious, and casts about her waist a golden girdle; finally, both send him home with a favouring breeze.

But, be it cave or palace, the home of the witch is that land of mystery, that Castle of Indolence in which the witch queen of folk-lore enslaves the sons of men—the house of the Hindu Tārā Bāī, the star maiden, who can neither grow old nor die, and the witchery of whose lulling songs no mortal can resist; the Horselberg into which Venus entices Tannhauser; the Ercildoune where the fairy queen enthralls Thomas the Rimer. We find the same situation in the Arabic tale of Ahmed and Peri Banou, in the Latin legend of Numa and Egeria. We may, again, compare the Celtic tale of Maildune, detained with his comrades by the island queen. They try to escape in a curragh; but the queen flings a thread towards them, which Maildune catches, and it clings to his hand. Then she draws them back, and they are detained nine months longer, every attempt which they make to escape being defeated in the same way. At last they begin to suspect that Maildune is a party to the trick, and they get another man to seize the thread. When he catches it they cut off his hand, and, plying their oars, pass away, while the isle rings with the lamentations of the queen and her maidens.[1]

Circe, the witch queen, turns the voyagers into beasts. Traces of Animism, as we have seen, appear in the epics, and people who believed in horses which weep and talk, would have no difficulty in accepting such cases of transformation. A good instance of these transformations is that of Jauharah, who spits in the face of

[1] Joyce, *Social History*, ii. 531; *Old Celtic Romances*, 152.

Badr Bāsim and turns him into a bird; or Queen Lāb: "Whoever entereth this city, being a young man like thyself, this miscreant witch taketh him, and he becometh a mule, or a horse, or an ass."[1] In one of the Russian tales the boy, by the enchantment of the witch, is turned into a kid, and in the Lorraine story of the *Fisherman's Son*, the witch strikes the hero with her wand, and turns into a tuft of grass himself, his horse, and his dog.[2] A parallel so remarkable to the tale of Circe occurs in the Buddhist Mahawanso that it is difficult not to suspect borrowing from the *Odyssey*. Here the Yakkhinī, an ogress, enthralls the comrades of Wijaya in a cave; he arms himself and goes to rescue them; she entices him to eat and drink, but he threatens her with his sword, and forces her to swear to cast no more spells; a feast follows, and he retires with her to a room which she causes to spring up at the foot of a tree.[3] In this and other seduction-tales of this class we seem to have an echo of the Matriarchate.

The myth of Scylla and Charybdis represents the cult of the whirlpool demon, a cruder variety of the tale of the Sirens. Scylla dwells in a cave turned towards Erebus; her voice is that of a new-born whelp; a dreadful monster is she; not even if a god met her would he behold her with gladness. She has twelve feet all dangling down, and six long necks, on each a hideous head, and therein three rows of teeth set thick and close, full of black death. She lies half concealed in her cave, and stretches out her arms to grope for dolphins or sea-dogs, or any other monstrous beast which deep-voiced Amphitrite feeds. Charybdis, again, under a great fig-tree in fullest leaf, sucks down

[1] Burton, *Nights*, vi. 77, 83.

[2] Gubernatis, *Zoological Mythology*, i. 209; Hartland, *Legend of Perseus*, i. 29.

[3] Tennent, *Ceylon*, i. 332 f.

her dark water. Thrice a day she sucks it in, and thrice spouts it out in terrible wise. "Far be thou from thence when she sucks in her water, for not the Earth-shaker himself might then save thee from thy bane."[1] Charybdis is thus more the actual, demoniacal whirlpool, while Scylla is a type of the monstrous water-beasts that drag men beneath the water, rend and devour them.

Scylla is connected with the dog, but Homer gives no support to the fancies of Vergil or Milton, who represent her extremities as ending in dogs. In a legend of this kind told in one of the Northern Sagas, the travellers reach a darkness which the eyes can scarcely pierce, and are exposed to a maelstrom which threatens to drag them down to chaos. Finally, they come quite unexpectedly to an island surrounded with a wall of rock, like that of Aeolus, containing subterranean caves, where giants lie concealed. At the entrances of these dwellings are tubs and vessels of gold. The adventurers take with them as much of the treasure as they can carry, and hasten to their ships. But the giants in the form of monstrous dogs rush after them, and tear one of the Frisians to pieces while the others escape.[2]

Charybdis, again, lives under a tree, and this is the place where the Hindu whirlpool spirit lurks. Thus we read: "Thus Satyavarta said, 'O Brahman! this is a banyan tree; under it they say that there is a gigantic whirlpool, the mouth of the subterranean fire, and we must take care in passing this way to avoid the spot; for those who enter that whirlpool never return again.'" Saktideva clings to the tree, as we are told Odysseus did, "like a bat," when he was saved from Charybdis, or as Sindibad did when he landed on the monstrous fish.[3]

In the stories of Autolycus and Sisyphus we seem to

[1] *Od.* xii. 85 ff. [2] Rydberg, *Teutonic Mythology*, 218.
[3] *Od.* xii. 432; Tawney, *Katha*, i. 220 f.; Burton, *Nights*, iv. 348.

have vague echoes of the cycle of the "Master Thief." In the *Iliad* Autolycus breaks into the well-builded house of Amyntor and steals his golden casque; while in the *Odyssey* we learn that he surpassed all men in knavery and skill in swearing, a gift conferred upon him by Hermes because he honoured him with an offering of the thighs of lambs and kids.[1] It was from Autolycus, his maternal grandfather, that Odysseus inherited his wiliness. In fact, his affiliation to the house of Laertes seems to be a later form of the tradition.[2] We may, perhaps, compare this robbery of the casque of Amyntor with that which Herodotus tells of Rhampsinitus and Pausanias of Trophonius and Agamedes, the Highland "Shifty Thief," or the Irish "Jack, the Cunning Thief."[3]

The other Homeric sharper is Sisyphus, if his name really means "the very wily one." He was, the poet tells us, the craftiest of men, and in calling him the son of Aiolos he has been supposed to imply that he belongs to the non-Hellenic area of the poems.[4] Homer does not tell us the nature of his crime. According to some he betrayed the designs of the gods; according to others he beguiled Persephone and made his escape from Hades; or, it is said, that he used to waylay travellers and slay them with a mighty stone. Another story tells that when Death came to carry him off he chained him; and Death being chained, no one died till Ares came and released Death. We have a parallel to this in the well-known tale of the innkeeper who shut up Death in a bottle.[5] Sisyphus may thus

[1] *Il.* x. 267 [iv.]; *Od.* xix. 394 f.

[2] *Od.* xi. 85, xix. 395.

[3] *Herod.* ii. 121; *Pausanias,* ix. 37, 3; Campbell, *Popular Tales,* i. 330 ff; Jacobs, *Celtic Folk Tales,* 224; Grimm, *Household Tales,* i. 431; Knowles, *Folk Tales of Kashmir,* 110, 338.

[4] *Il.* vi. 153 [ii. A].

[5] Crane, *Italian Popular Tales,* 215 ff.; Grimm, *Teutonic Mythology,* ii. 854.

be compared with Gambling Hansel in the German tale, with Billy Dawson in the Irish story of the *Three Wishes*, and with Conan in the Finn Saga, who harries hell.[1]

In the stories of Sisyphus and Tantalus, it is specially to be noted that their punishment is quite inconsistent with the Homeric tradition of the underworld, in which there is no trace of retribution after death. The Homeric religion, says Miss Harrison,[2] "was too easy-going, too essentially aristocratic, to provide an eternity even of torture for the religious figures it degraded and despised. Enough for it if they were carelessly banished to their own proper kingdom, the underworld." Hence these tales are probably late additions to the *Nekuia*, and there is much to be said for the suggestion that Sisyphus is a disestablished sun-god, banished to the nether world, which, like the sun, he visits daily only to rise again with the dawn. It may be remembered in this connexion that Helios himself threatens to go down and shine among the dead if Zeus will not avenge his wrongs.[3] This, then, is one of the few Homeric puzzles which may be solved by the methods of the mythological school of interpreters. The ball which he rolls up the slope may represent the sun's course in the heavens, which we know was in other mythologies pictured in the same way.[4]

It is much more difficult to grasp the idea which lies behind the myth of Tantalus. It is almost certain that it is a late addition to the *Nekuia*, because Homer uses a comparatively modern version of the story. The archaic tale told that Tantalus suffered not in hell, but in heaven, where he was admitted to the table of the gods. Zeus promised to grant him his heart's desire, and he willed

[1] Grimm, *Household Tales*, i. 322 ff.; Campbell, *The Fians*, 73; Jacobs, *Celtic Folk Tales*, 266 f.; Frazer, *Pausanias*, ii. 33.

[2] *Prolegomena*, 613.

[3] *Od.* xii. 382.

[4] Cox, *Introduction*, 7 ff.; Rhys, *Hibbert Lectures*, 453.

to live for ever like the gods. Zeus gave him the boon of immortality, but he hung a great stone over him, which, like the sword of Damocles, prevented him from enjoying the banquet spread before him.[1] In the Homeric version of the story, as in the case of Sisyphus, the poet does not describe the sin for which he was condemned to grievous torment, unable to drink the water or touch the fruits which seemed to be within his grasp until the wind tossed them to the clouds.[2] The older story possibly points to a clash of rival cults, and Tantalus may be a degraded sun-god, striving to grasp the waters which dry up before the splendour of his rays. For his punishment we may perhaps compare the American famine-giant, who hangs from the lodge-pole with his head just touching the ground;[3] or more closely the Norse myth of the Jutlander who broke the water-jug of King Cnut: "He met with his reward. He became mad, and suffered from burning thirst, and one day having laid himself down by a spring to draw up water, he slipt halfway down into the water, and remained hanging by his legs, though without touching it, and so died."[4] The same fate is reserved in the Buddhist hell for those who are miserly, covetous, uncharitable, or gluttonous.[5]

Another of these broken-down sun myths probably appears in the tale of the Planktai or Wandering Rocks. "By this way even winged things may never pass, not even the cowering doves that bear ambrosia to Father Zeus; but the sheer rock evermore takes one of these away, and the Father sends another to make up the tale."[6] The story has been explained in various ways—as a tradition of icebergs seen by mariners in the northern seas; by the actual appearance of some islands in the

[1] Frazer, *Pausanias*, v. 392.

[2] *Od.* xi. 582 f.

[3] Schoolcraft, *Notes on the Iroquois*, 154.

[4] Thorpe, *Northern Mythology*, ii. 226.

[5] Waddell, *Buddhism of Tibet*, 96 f.

[6] *Od.* xii. 61 ff.

Bosporus, parts of which are occasionally submerged in stormy weather, or which seem to meet and separate again as a ship passes between them.[1] On the other hand, the sun is supposed by many races to pass through two rocks always opening and shutting, and by this route the spirit has to pass to gain its rest.[2] Among the Egyptians this fancy of the road of the soul was very fully developed, and they had a myth which closely resembles that of Homer. Every year, they said, all the herons assemble at the mountain now called Gebel-et-ter. One after another they plunge their beaks into the cleft of the hill until it closes on one of them; and then forthwith all the others fly away. But the bird that has been caught struggles until it dies, and there its body lies till it has fallen into dust, an obvious reminiscence of the mountain cleft at Abydus, whereby the souls must pass in the form of human-headed birds in order to reach the other world.[3] In a Russian tale the hero is sent to find the Water of Life from between two mountains which fly apart for three minutes every day. His horse's hind legs are caught by the rocks, but the water revives him; in another tale of the same kind the hare passing through rocks like these loses her tail, and since then hares have no tails to speak of.[4] Of rocks that close and open at a word, as in the tale of *Ali Baba and the Forty Thieves,* the instances in folklore are legion.[5]

Of much the same class is the myth of the Floating Island in which Aeolus dwelt.[6] The idea was familiar

[1] See Crantz, *History of Greenland*, i. 24 f.

[2] Tylor, *Primitive Culture*,[2] i. 347 ff.; cf. Gill, *Myths and Songs of the S. Pacific*, quoted by Monro, *Odyssey*, ii. 293.

[3] Maspero, *Life in Ancient Egypt*, 141; *Dawn of Civilisation*, 10 n.

[4] McCulloch, *Childhood of Fiction*, 59; Miss Cox, *Introduction*, 268.

[5] Miss Cox, *Cinderella*, 499 f.; Grimm, *Teutonic Mythology*, ii. 971 f.; *id. Household Tales*, ii. 439; Rhys, *Celtic Folk-lore* i. 254.

[6] *Od.* x. 3.

to the Greeks in the case of Delos, but even the credulity of Herodotus hesitated at the account of the floating island of Chemmis.[1] Some have supposed that the floating island of Aeolus was an iceberg; but in view of the wide provenance of the legend this seems inadequate. We have the story in the case of Disco Island, which two Eskimos towed with the hair of a little child, chanting a magical lay, and anchored it where it now stands.[2] The Japanese tell the same tale of Onogoro; and in the Celtic story Balor directs his men to fix a cable round the isle of Erinn and sail with it home out of the reach of the De Danaan, as Brian draws the sunken isle of Fiucarn out of the depths of the sea.[3]

Aeolus is the wizard who has the winds in his keeping. Laamao-mao is the Hawaian Aeolus, from whose calabash winds come at his bidding.[4] Oddi, the Danish admiral, could raise a storm against his enemies, and Hraesvelg was the storm-giant of Scandinavia, who could shake the winds out of his bag.[5] In Irish tradition the Druids of the De Danaan can raise a wind which blows a fleet to sea; the wind prophets of Samoa and the Solomon Islands can bring wind and rain, and to this day women in Lerwick earn their living by selling winds to sailors.[6]

The tale of the Phaeacians is of peculiar interest. Some have seen in it a prototype of "a long series of imaginings, which with various degrees of bitterness or of gentle irony have reflected some features or some tendencies of contemporary life, or have embodied a contemporary

[1] *Od.* ii. 156.

[2] Rink, *Tales and Traditions*, 464.

[3] Joyce, *Old Celtic Romances*, 41, 87; Rhys, *Celtic Folk-lore*, i. 90.

[4] Fornander, *An Account of the Polynesian Race*, ii. 53.

[5] Thorpe, *Northern Mythology*, i. 215, 218, ii. 193, iii. 23; *Saxo*, ed. Elton-Powell, 156; Grimm, *Teutonic Mythology*, ii. 640, iii. 1057.

[6] O'Curry, *Manners and Customs*, ii. 189; Guppy, *Solomon Islands*, 55; Turner, *Samoa*, 320, 462; Rogers, *Social Life in Scotland*, iii. 220; cf. Frazer, *Golden Bough*,[2] i. 119 ff.

ideal, such as More's *Utopia*, Swift's *Laputa*, or Johnson's *Rasselas*. All grosser elements are purged away; humanity appears in the most engaging aspect; and yet in the complacency of this island folk, in their imagined security, their pride of ships, their boast of nearness to the gods, it seems allowable to trace some good-humoured persiflage of the poet's own neighbours, whom, to avoid offending them, he has purposely located on a distant and imaginary shore."[1] In short, he is supposed to have placed at Corcyra, which can in no wise be compared with it, the cultured, luxurious people of the Ionian coast. If the tale has a basis of fact, it may be a reminiscence of the Minoan civilisation. At the same time, it is clear that the Phaeacians are in the land of faery. Gerland long ago compared the Phaeacian episode with the tale of Saktideva in Somadeva's collection.[2] He, like Odysseus, is saved from a whirlpool by clinging to the tree which overhangs it; he is carried to the Golden City, and entertained by the Vidhyādharī or fairy queen, who is destined to wed a mortal. But as in the beautiful account of Nausikaa, her lover deserts her and returns to marry his old love.[3]

An attempt, again, has been made to compare this ideal Phaeacian world with the Northern legend of the Ferrymen of Death, who, as Procopius tells us, convey the souls of the departed to the Isle of Brittia.[4] But this gloomy tale is ill suited to the Phaeacians, who live an easy, joyous life, devoid of care, in no sense akin to the gloomy denizens of the lower world. Their ships are the magic vessels of which there are many examples in legend—the enchanted ship of the Highland tale, which can sail on sea or land; Gonachry, the "heart-wounder," which bears the hero in search of the

[1] Campbell, *Religion in Greek Literature*, 88.

[2] Monro, *Odyssey*, ii. 293.

[3] Tawney, *Katha*, i. 194 ff.

[4] Rhys, *Celtic Folk-lore*, ii. 439 f.

White Swan of the Smooth Neck, whom he loves; the magic bone on which Oller, the mighty Norse wizard, sails across the deep; Odinn's bark, Skidvladner, which can be folded up as a napkin, and when her sails are set a favouring breeze arising wafts her to whatever shore the helmsman wills.[1] So the Edda tells of the ship, Naglfar, which is to be built of the parings of dead men's nails, and hence they held it a sacred duty to cut the nails of the corpse, because both men and gods dread the coming of this awful bark.[2] In short, these magical conveyances, like the carpet of Solomon, the wooden horse of the *Arabian Nights*, the flying image of the bird Garuda in Hindu tradition, are common to the folk-lore of the whole world, and the origin of many of them may be traced to the magic ships which early fancy saw in the racing clouds or the hailstorm drifting across the sky.

The Saga of the Wooden Horse, in which the warriors are concealed, appears only in the *Odyssey*,[3] and forms part of a wide cycle of tradition. Perhaps the earliest form of the tale is to be found in the Egyptian story of the *Taking of Joppa*, and the Arab plan for the capture of Edessa, which was framed on similar lines, is said to have failed owing to the suspicions of the Governor of the city.[4] The best modern instance is that of Ali Baba, where the robber captain and his comrades conceal themselves in oil jars, and are detected by the wit of the slave girl, Morgiana.[5] In a variant from Cyprus the black men are concealed by the ogre

[1] Campbell, *Popular Tales*, i. 257: Macdougall-Nutt, *Folk and Hero Tales*, 289; MacInnes-Nutt, *Waifs and Strays*, 449; *Saxo*, ed. Elton-Powell, 99; Rydberg, *Teutonic Mythology*, 24; Mallet, *Northern Antiquities*, 435.

[2] Grimm, *Teutonic Mythology*, ii. 814; Rydberg, *op. cit.* 379; Mallet, *op. cit.* 452.

[3] *Od.* iv. 271 f.; viii. 502 ff.; xi. 523 ff.

[4] Petrie, *Egyptian Tales*, ii. 1 ff.

[5] Burton, *Nights*, x. 209 ff.

in bales, and in Sicily Ohime, the ogre, hides in a hollow statue of silver which he causes to be introduced into the room of the heroine.[1] Besides this class of story, which may be called the "Robber Chief" type, there are two others, one of which Shakespeare uses in *Cymbeline*, derived from Boccaccio, where the traitor lover conceals himself in the lady's chamber, and notes a mark on her breast whereby he deludes her husband into suspecting her honour.[2] The other type of the story is even more widely spread, and may be called the "Princess of Balkh," which belongs to the "Bride Wager" group, in which the youngest of the brothers finds the princess by entering her palace concealed in a lion of gold and silver, which appears in the Sicilian version in the shape of the "Musical Eagle."[3] Of these types there are numerous variants, as in the Magyar tale of the hero who enters the palace concealed in a silver horse, or in the Hindu story of the "King of Vatsa," who is attacked by warriors hidden in an artificial elephant.[4] In the Celtic tale, Brandruff conceals his warriors covered over with provisions in great hampers laden on oxen, and these he drives into the camp of the King of Ireland, whom he overcomes.[5] Even at the present day the capture of many famous Hindu forts is said to have been effected by introducing warriors in female guise concealed in litters.[6] In countries where women are secluded this device may often have

[1] *Folk-lore Record*, iii. pt. ii. 185 f.; *Folk-lore Journal*, iii. 206 ff.

[2] *Decameron*, Day ii. Tale 9; Hazlitt, *Shakespeare's Library*, i. pt. ii. 179.

[3] *Punjab Notes and Queries*, iv. 48: Pitrè, *Biblioteca*, v. 307.

[4] Jones-Kropf, *Magyar Folk Tales*, 139 f.; Geldart, *Folk-lore of Modern Greece*, 98; Tawney, *Katha*, i. 72.

[5] Joyce, *Social History*, i. 141.

[6] Tod, *Annals of Rajasthan*, i. 252, 665; *Journal Asiatic Society of Bengal*, lxii. 13.

been practised with success, and the whole cycle may be based on some historical incidents.

Closely connected with this Saga is that of the "Disguised Deserter," who maims himself, as Odysseus did, and makes his way into the enemy's camp.[1] This also may be of historical origin. Herodotus tells the same tale of the Zopyrus, who feigned himself to be a deserter from the Persian army, and enabled Darius to capture Babylon; of Peisistratus, who by a similar device secured a bodyguard and became tyrant of Athens; the same plan was repeated to complete the ruin of the army of the Emperor Julian.[2] We have a variant of these disguise stories in the return of Odysseus as a beggar, an incident which is constantly reproduced in the later folk-tales.[3]

I must bring this paper to a close with the final tragedy which ends the story of the siege of Troy. I have been able to discuss only a small portion of the folk-lore and archaic beliefs which are embedded in the epics. The result, I venture to think, is only to increase our admiration of the great writer who has wedded these incidents to the noblest verse. We honour him not only as the first of European folk-lorists, but as the first and noblest writer who devoted his genius to the record of beliefs and traditions which it is the task of this Society to collect and interpret.

W. CROOKE.

[1] *Od.* iv. 244 ff.

[2] *Herod.* iii. 154, i. 59; Gibbon, *Decline and Fall*, iii. 206; Frazer, *Pausanias*, iii. 413.

[3] Grimm, *Household Tales*, i. 406.

Folk-Lore.

TRANSACTIONS OF THE FOLK-LORE SOCIETY.

VOL. XI.] MARCH, 1900. [No. I.

THE LEGENDS OF KRISHNA.

BY W. CROOKE, B.A.

(*Read at Meeting of 21st June, 1899.*)

THE cycle of folklore and popular belief which centres round Krishna, one of the most important elements in the neo-Brâhmanical creed of modern India, forms an interesting chapter in the development of Hindu religious myth and cultus. This neo-Brâhmanism is now the working faith which controls the spiritual destinies of two hundred and seven millions of people. It is a faith without a definite creed, with no church, no pope, no convocation. It is the most catholic of the old world religions, providing as it does for the needs of jungle-folk on the borderland of savagery and for those most keen-witted of religious disputants, the Vedantists of Mathura or Benares. It is a great missionary religion, working not in the way with which we are familiar, through societies and an organised body of teachers, but by the agency of shock-headed Jogis and ash-covered Sannyâsis. It is one of the most catholic of faiths, because though it has many gods it enforces the worship of no one deity on any of its members.

Hence for the purpose of estimating the prevalence of different forms of Hindu belief statistics are of little value.

At the last census each person was asked to name the god which he usually worshipped; but this does not exclude the possibility that he may worship more than one. On the contrary, it is certain that to meet the varying needs of his life he combines the belief in his personal god with that of others, few or many. The basis of his belief is animistic, but he supplements this form of worship by the casual or periodical veneration of one or several of the members of the official pantheon. When we find, then, that five and a half millions of people in the Panjab and North-Western Provinces professed devotion to Krishna, we may assume that a very much larger number revere him as a member of the class of deities which are known generally as Vaishnava, or grouped round the personality of Vishnu.

This is not the place or time to discuss in detail the historical development of the cult; but a few words must be said on this point as an introduction to the consideration of his legends, which is the special subject of this paper.

He is, to begin with, a comparatively new god, that is to say, he does not appear in the Vedas. We first hear of Krishna, son of Devakî, in the Chhândogya Upanishad, one of the supplements to the Sâma Veda, which are clearly later than the Sanhitas or Brâhmanas, and in their present recension embody the views of that school of philosophical Brâhmanism which is of course separated by a long interval from that of the nature worship embodied in the earlier hymns. Krishna is here only a scholar, eager in the pursuit of knowledge, and perhaps a member of the military caste.[1] Passing on to the Epic period, in the Mahâbhârata, which was probably composed between the time of the Greek traveller Megasthenes (306—295 B.C.) and the second half of the first century of our era,[2] we find that Krishna occupies a higher place, but still his divinity is not fully assured. Râma and Krishna are here at once gods

[1] Weber, *History of Indian Literature*, 71.
[2] *Ibid.*, 186.

and men. They are accepted as incarnations of Vishnu, but at the same time they are regarded as human heroes, acting under the influence of human motives, and taking no advantage of their divine supremacy. Krishna even worships Siva and wins boons from him.[1] Later additions to and interpolations in the text of the Epics assert his divinity; and in particular this view of his nature finds expression in the celebrated philosophical poem known as the Bhâgavadgîta, which is obviously a late supplement to the Mahâbhârata. The same view was again enforced and extended in the Hari-vansa, and especially in the Bhâgavata Purâna, which may be as late as the tenth or eleventh century of our era.

It is impossible, then, to assign a definite date to a cultus thus gradually developed, as we are able to do in the case of other great historical religions, Buddhism, Islâm, or Christianity. There seems, however, good reason to suspect that the elevation of Krishna to divine honours was coincident with the rise of the neo-Brâhmanism on the decay of Buddhism. The older Brâhmanism was too esoteric, too much the faith of priests and nobles, to influence the masses. In this respect Brâhmanism learned a lesson from Buddhism, and with a view to popularise its tenets adopted not only the cult of the Saktî, or female element, which may have been one of the indigenous idolatries, but also drew within its fold some of the local or tribal gods, of whom, as we shall see, Krishna was probably one. Nay more, it has been conjectured that in this new alliance it was not Vishnu, but Krishna, who was the predominant partner, and that it was by its combination with the Krishna or other allied cult that Vaishnavism finally won its way to the affections of the masses in Northern India.

It is outside my present purpose to discuss how far the

[1] Muir, *Original Sanskrit Texts*, iv., 169, 182 *seqq.* ; Wilson-Hall, *Vishnu Purâna*, i., intro., xv. For a summary of the story of Krishna, see Mahâbhârata, *Drona Parva*, sec. ii., trans. Ray, v., 31 *seqq.*

new revelation may have owed its inspiration to Christian or other Western influence. It has been supposed that on the one hand Buddhism profoundly influenced the Western Church, and the analogies between Lamaism in Tibet and the ritual and organisation of the Roman Catholic Church have attracted the attention of many observers. It has been supposed again that the episode in the Mahâbhârata where Nârada the Saint visits Sweta-dwîpa, "the White Island," implies early relations between Brâhmanism and Alexandrian Christianity.[1] I need hardly dwell upon the indications in the Krishna mythus, presently to be related, which suggest the same inference. The question has, however, hardly yet been settled to the satisfaction of scholars,[2] and in any case it would lead me too far from the special subject of this paper.

I pass on to the popular traditions concerning Krishna.[3]

To put the story as briefly as possible, we find a branch of the great Yâdava clan of Kshatriyas, who probably owed their origin to a Yu-echi invasion from Central Asia, settled on the banks of the River Jumna, with Mathura as their capital. That they were outsiders or new-comers is important when we come to consider certain elements in the cultus which indicate foreign influence. Krishna, we are told, was the son of Vasu-deva and Devakî. The former, by one interpretation of his name, is one of the old celestial genii, "the bright ones"; the latter, Devakî, "the divine one," has been identified with the seductive water-nymph of folklore. But more probably in Devakî and Krishna we may see representatives of the world-wide group of the divine mother and the fateful child—Nana of Babylon, Isis and Horus in Egypt, Lucina and her child in Latin tradition.

[1] Weber, *Indische Studien*, i., 400, ii., 168; Frazer, *Literary History of India*, 231; Ray, *Mahâbhârata*, viii., 752.

[2] See Dutt, *Ancient India*, ii., 276.

[3] The most accessible authorities are Growse, *Mathura, a District Memoir* Allahabad, 1883; Lallu Lâl, *Prem Sâgar*, translated by E. B. Eastwick.

At the time of the birth of Krishna we find the rightful king, Ugrasena, like so many savage half-priests, half-monarchs, when their power of controlling the deities becomes abated, deposed by his son, the usurper Kamsa. He, we are told, cruelly persecuted his rivals, an incident in which some have recognised a conflict of cults, and some have gone so far as to call Kamsa a Jaina, an opponent of the neo-Vaishnava faith. However this may be, Krishna, who was a cousin of the usurper, defeated and slew him and restored Ugrasena to the throne. But his triumph did not last long. He was himself attacked by the father-in-law of Kamsa, Jarasandha, king of Magadha or Bihâr, who was allied with a monarch known as Kala-yavana, the Ionian or Greek, who may have been a king of Kâshmîr or one of the Bactrian descendants of the Great Alexander. Krishna, we learn, was forced to abandon Mathura and retire to Dwâraka on the Gulf of Kachh, where, after various adventures, including his interposition on the side of the Pândavas in the great war recorded in the Mahâbhârata, by which their success was assured, he is said to have been slain, and his bones, according to later Brâhmanical tradition, rest inside the famous idol at Jaggan-nâth.

From a saga like this, obviously the work of many hands and embodying many variant traditions, it is hopeless to sift any historical facts. Krishna may have been a local hero of the Yâdava clan of Kshatriyas; they may have brought with them some part of his cultus from their home in Central Asia; they may have absorbed parts of it from the indigenous idolatries; his tale may suggest a conflict between more than one rival faith. For the sober historian it possesses little more value than the myths of the Arthurian cycle. To one school of mythologists, of course, the whole story is only a solar myth.

We are perhaps on safer ground when we suggest that round a single figure, which may possibly be historical, the cultus, as we find it, may be the result of that syncretism which is so familiar an agency in the growth of religious belief. He may, in other words, be only a figure-head round which local myths have centred, like Alexander or Karl the Great. In the case of the Greek Apollo, for instance, the wolf, the ram, the dolphin, the mouse, the laurel probably represent so many variant cults, some of them possibly totemistic, which came to be grouped round and identified with one dominant divine personage. When from this point of view we come to examine the Krishna mythus we find his connection with cattle specially prominent. His most popular titles are Govinda and Gopâla, "the cowherd;" and as a protector of kine he may be readily compared with similar deities in other parts of the world. Thus, in Greece we have Apollo Nomios, and in another shape Krishna as Murli-dhara, "the flute-player," reminds us of Apollo Mousegetes, the leader of the Muses, the patron of music and song. So in Greece and Rome, Hermes and Pan, Pales and Priapus, Faunus and Lupercus, Bubona and Epona, and possibly the Babylonian Eabani,[1] are in various forms the deities who give increase to the flocks and protect domestic animals from wild beasts and other dangers—a cult in no sense primitive, but based on the needs of a society in which cattle-breeding and husbandry are already well advanced. From this point of view he has his kinsfolk in the local divinities of modern India—Siddhua and Buddhua, Nâgar-deo, Chaumu, Kaluva and Bîr-nâth, who shield the herds from harm.[2] So his brother Bala-râma seems to have been an old agricultural god known as Halabrit, "the plough-bearer," with the lustful temper of Pan or Silenus, just as Sîtâ, "the furrow," was embodied in the Râma myth. He may thus in his most primitive form have been an old cattle god adopted into the Brâhmanical pantheon,

[1] Maspero, *Dawn of Civilisation*, 576.

[2] Crooke, *Popular Religion and Folklore of Northern India*, ii., 81 *seqq.*; *Tribes and Castes of the North-Western Provinces and Oudh*, i., 63 *seqq.*

like Siva in his form as Pasupa or Pasupati, "the lord of kine," especially of those set apart for sacrifice.

We may even go further and suggest a conflict of rival agricultural cults. Krishna elopes with Rukminî, "the golden," the betrothed of Sisupâla, whom he encounters and decapitates with his discus. Now Sisupâla means "cherisher of the young," in particular of young animals, the equivalent of the Greek Kourotrophos, the guardian deity of the springs near which the hair of youths and maidens was dedicated. In this view he too would be another rural deity of the same kind.

Like that of so many gods, the birth of Krishna was in wondrous wise. A supernatural voice, what the Greeks would have called a Phemê, announced to the usurper Kamsa that his slayer would be born in the eighth son of his kinsman Vasudeva and Devakî, niece of the deposed monarch Ugrasena. To defeat the prophecy, Kamsa summoned the pair to Mathura and kept them in ward. Each of their children as it was born was destroyed. But when Devakî became pregnant for the seventh time the embryo was miraculously transferred to the womb of Rohinî, "the red cow," the second wife of Vasudeva, and it was reported that Devakî had miscarried. In due time the fated child was born and was named Sankarshana, "he that was taken from the womb of his mother," and later on Balarâma, or Baladeva, who aided his brother Krishna in overthrowing the tyrant. With this we may compare the many folktales which tell of the birth of the fateful child, and it is needless to suggest the obvious analogy to the tale of Herod.[1]

We have, again, here an instance of the common case of a duality of gods—the Asvins, the Dioscuri, Yama and Yamî, Romulus and Remus, Epimetheus and Prometheus, indicating either syncretism, the combination of rival cults,

[1] Compare the Slavonic versions, *Journal of the Anthropological Institute*, xxi., 456 *seqq.*, and the legend of the birth of the successors of the Egyptian Kheops, Maspero, *loc. cit.*, 386 *seqq.*

or perhaps in the cases where male and female deities are grouped in pairs the idea of the world of sense developed by the normal connection of the sexes.

Here, too, we have the familiar case of the god or hero born in some abnormal way. Often he is motherless or unborn or springs from his father alone, as Athena from the thigh of Zeus, which suggests the couvade, or the mother is delivered by the Cæsarean operation. One or other of such incidents presents itself in the tales of Dionysus, Asklepios, Lychas, Sakya-muni, Tristram, Macduff, Dubrune Nikititsch, and Sigfried.[1]

But the tale of the transfer of the embryo from one mother to the other is more unusual, and several threads of folk belief seem to be combined which is not easy to disentangle. To begin with, abnormal birth is regarded as auspicious, for instance, in the Hindu belief that children born by the foot presentation are lucky.[2] Next, we have the common belief in the possibility of birth transference, where by cutting off part of a child's clothes, soaking it in water and drinking it, causes a barren woman to conceive, or the Chinese theory that the soul of a great man is incarnated in one of the women who watch his funeral.[3] The Aruntas of Australia, as described by Messrs. Spencer and Gillen, have adopted this as the normal explanation of the fact of conception. We meet similar cases of interference with and transfer of the embryo in the legend of Indra, who fearing that Aditî would bear a child superior to himself, entered her womb and cut the fœtus into forty-nine pieces; of the child born at Kausambi, swallowed by a fish and carried to Benares, where he is adopted by the wife of a nobleman and recognised by his true mother; when the case comes to be

[1] Ploss, *Das Weib*, ii., 405, 407; Grimm, *Teutonic Mythology* (trans. Stallybrass), i., 385; Elton-Powell, *Saxo Grammaticus*, intro., lxiv.

[2] *Panjab Notes and Queries*, iii., 78.

[3] *Ibid.*, iii., 116. Hartland, *Legend of Perseus*, i., 160; Frazer, *Golden Bough*, i., 239.

tried by the king he decides that the child belongs to both mothers, to one by maternity, to the other by adoption, and hence it was called Bakula, "he of the two septs"; of Buddhasatva, who entered into Chandra-devî and was conceived of her.[1]

So we have triple maternity in the tale of Siva in his form as Tryambaka, "he who has three mothers,"[2] as Dionysus was Dimetor, the Bimatris of Ovid.[3] In the same way Heimdall was the son of nine mothers, giantesses. Reinhart, after the Cæsarean operation, was brought to birth in the stomachs of newly-slaughtered swine, and Agni was the son of many mothers.[4] A further development occurs in the tales of adoption, as that of Herakles and Hera, where the adopting mother goes through the farce of a simulated birth, which Diodorus tells us was a practice of the barbarians of his time.[5] In the *Legenda Aurea* we read of the birth of Judas, announced to be a fateful child, exposed and taken up by the queen of the Isle Scarioth, who simulates pregnancy, and represents the recovered child to be her own.[6] Lastly, it has passed into modern folklore in the tale of Seven Mothers and their Son,[7] naturally suggested by the conditions of a polygamous household.

All the fateful children of the folktales have miraculous powers at birth. Otus and Ephialtes, another case of dualism, who were born of monstrous size;[8] the new-born Apollo, who in the Homeric hymn, when he tastes the nectar and ambrosia, leaps from his swaddling clothes,

[1] *Journal of the Asiatic Society*, Bengal, xxxiv., 226; Ward, *Hindoos*, ii., 55, 395.

[2] Barth, *Religions of India*, 161.

[3] *Metam.*, iv., 12.

[4] Grimm, *loc. cit.*, i., 234, 389; Rig Veda, iii., 23, 3; x., 45, 2; i., 141, 2; also compare the story of the birth of Huitzilopochtli, Bancroft, *Native Races*, iii., 310 *seqq.*

[5] Hartland, *loc. cit.*, ii., 419.

[6] Cap. xlv., a reference for which I am indebted to Mr. Hartland.

[7] Temple-Steel, *Wideawake Stories*, 98 *seqq.*

[8] *Odyssey*, xi., 305 *seqq.*

begins to speak, and wanders through the land; Vali, in the Norse tale, when one night old sallies out to avenge the death of Balder; and Magni, son of Thor by the giantess Jarnsaxa, when three nights old flings off the giant's foot with which the monster would have crushed his father.[1] So the Dayaks have a like marvellous child in Seragunting; and Robert the Devil, we are told, bit off his nurse's paps and overpowered all the children of his age; while Tom Hickathrift "at ten years old was six feet high and three feet across, with a hand like a shoulder of mutton, and everything else proportionable." [2] As St. Benedict sang Eucharistic hymns before he was born, so in the Zulu folktale there is a child who speaks in the womb of his mother; the Kafir Simbukumbukwana speaks on the day of his birth; and the Hindu heroine, Somaprabhâ, talks the moment she is born.[3] Thus this long series of precocious imps passes on to the boy Cadi of the *Arabian Nights* and the Enfant Terrible of our *Punch*.[4]

The feats of the infant Krishna are of the usual class. He upsets a waggon loaded with pails of milk; when he is tethered to a big wooden mortar he drags it away with him; he pulls down monstrous trees; and so on.[5] As a good example of the evolution of myth the last miracle has been localised at Girnâr in Kâthiâwâr, with the Brâhmanic gloss that the trees were really divine personages compelled by a curse of some saint to enter the form of trees till they were uprooted by Krishna, the merciful saviour.[6]

[1] Grimm, *loc. cit.*, i., 320 *seqq*.

[2] Ling Roth, *Natives of Sarawak*, i., 198 *seqq*.; Hazlitt, *National Tales*, 59, 431.

[3] Callaway, *Nursery Tales*, i., 6; Theal, *Kaffir Folklore*, 73; Tawney, *Katha Sarit Sâgara*, i., 119, 156. The child of Mamatâ speaks in the womb, *Mahâbhârata*, *Adi Parva*, sec. 104, Ray trans., i., 314.

[4] Burton, *Arabian Nights* (Library Edition), x., 243; Clouston, *Popular Tales and Fictions*, ii., 12 *seqq*.; Miss Stokes, *Indian Fairy Tales*, 279 *seqq*.

[5] Growse, *loc. cit.*, 55 *seqq*.; Wilson-Hall, *loc. cit.*, iv., 279 *seqq*.

[6] *Bombay Gazetteer*, viii., 441 *seqq*.

Krishna again appears as a slayer of dragons and monsters. Like all great cycles of myth, that of the worm-slayer seems to be founded on more than one train of thought. In one phase, as in the defeat of Ahi or Vritra by Indra, or in the legend of Imra as told by the Kâfirs of the Hindu Kush, it is a pure nature-myth. The snake, like the frog or lizard of many savage mythologies, swallows the waters, which are released when the monster is destroyed. Again, while the theory advanced by some writers[1] that the myth is a reminiscence of the struggles of early man with some

> "Dragons of the prime
> That tare each other in their slime,"

is opposed to all the conclusions of palæontology, on the other hand the tale may in some cases be based on the discovery of the gigantic bones of some extinct saurian. One famous group of tales of this class, that in which the hero slays the dragon which demands a human victim, an impostor appears and claims the reward, the trick being discovered by the production of the tongue or some other part of the slaughtered dragon, probably, as Mr. Hartland shows,[2] points to a reaction against an early custom of offering a victim to some water spirit conceived in dragon form.

But in many cases the myth seems to represent a conflict of rival cults. Such, for instance, seems to be the most reasonable explanation of the slaughter of the python by Apollo. Here the dragon may be associated with the worship of Ge or some of the other chthonic powers, which was overthrown by the new-comer god. In other cases, as in that of Athena associated with the earth-snake, Erechtheus-Erichthonios, we may suspect the fusion of

[1] Gould, *Mythical Monsters*, chap. vi.

[2] Hartland, *loc. cit.*, iii., 66 *seqq.*; Frazer, *Pausanias*, i., 476; ii., 528; v., 60, 143.

divergent cults. The fact, again, that some of our English dragons, like those of Sockburn or Wantley, where the dragon has been euphemised into a roguish attorney, have their home on a hill or prehistoric tumulus, suggests that some cult of the dead may be at the root of the matter. When the myth became Christianised, the overthrow of rival beliefs becomes more obvious, as in the case of St. George, St. Patrick, and St. Mac Creiche in Ireland, St. Philip, who slew the dragon of Hierapolis, St. Martha and the Tarasque dragon in Provence, St. Florent and the dragon of the Loire, St. Cado, St. Maudet and St. Pol in Brittany, St. Keyne in Cornwall, St. O'Heany and the Banagher worm, and many others.[1]

The monster-slaying feats of Krishna are of various kinds. One day the children of the herdsmen were playing and entered what they supposed to be a cave in the rocks, but which was really the expanded jaws of the serpent king, Aghâsura. He drew a deep breath and sucked them in, but Krishna bade them be of good cheer, and swelled his body to such a size that the serpent burst, and all the children stepped out unharmed.[2] Here we have the common myth of the swallowing and the disgorging, which appears in the tale of Jonah and the whale, that of Kronos and Herakles, and all through savage folklore.[3]

On another occasion an immense boa-constrictor seized Nanda, Krishna's foster-father, on which the youthful god set his foot on the head of the monster, which was forthwith transformed into a lovely youth. For, ages before, a Ganymede of the Court of Heaven, Sudarshan by name, in his insolence danced before Angiras, the sage. The holy

[1] Maury, *Essai sur les légendes pieuses du Moyen Age*, 144; 1st Series *Notes and Queries*, vi., 147, 519; 3rd Series, ix., 29, 158; 8th Series, vi., 113; 2nd Series, viii., 509; Tezcatlipoca in Mexico, Bancroft, *loc. cit.*, iii., 283.

[2] Growse, *loc. cit.*, 57.

Lang, *Myth, Ritual, and Religion* (2nd ed.), i., 295.

man, who by the force of his austerities was able to overcome the gods themselves, in his wrath cursed him that he should become a snake, and remain in that loathly shape till the advent of the gracious Krishna.[1]

Again, while Krishna is bathing, he is attacked by Kâliya, "the black one," the dragon of the River Jumna, the personified spirit of the waters, which in so many tales, that of Narcissus for instance, drags down the beautiful hero into the gloomy depths. Krishna crushed the head of the monster, and would have slain him had not the dragon's wives come out of the water and implored him to take pity on their spouse. Krishna forgave him, adding that he should ever bear upon his brow the impress of the divine feet and be thus safe from his enemies,[2] one of the many myths invented to explain the marks on the bodies of beasts and birds—the blood on Robin Redbreast, the mottled plumage of the Indian black partridge, the stripes upon the back of the little house squirrel.[3]

Like Herakles and so many heroes of the folktales, Krishna overcomes other monsters and demons. Thus, when the demon Bachhâsura, in the form of a mighty crane, gobbled up the herd-boys, Krishna allowed himself to be devoured with them; but he proved so hot a mouthful that the demon was only too glad to drop him. Then the divine youth seized the brute by his long bill, and rent him in twain.[4] So with the demon Dhenuka, who found the boys plucking fruit from his palm-trees, and, taking the form of an ass, kicked Balarâma on the breast. But Balarâma hurled him so high that he fell on the top of one of the tallest trees and caused the fruit to fall in abundance.[5] The monster, as in the case of Jack and the

[1] Growse, *loc. cit.*, 61.

[2] *Ibid.*, 57 *seqq.*; Wilson-Hall, *loc. cit.*, iv., 286 *seqq.*

[3] Crooke, *Popular Religion and Folklore of Northern India*, ii., 242, 251.

[4] Growse, *loc. cit.*, 57.

[5] *Ibid.*, 55; Wilson-Hall, *loc. cit.*, iv., 297 *seqq.*

Beanstalk, is always fair game, and it is rather a respectable act to plunder him.

Again, the demon Pralamba, disguising himself as a youth, challenges Krishna and his companions to race. Balarâma mounted on the shoulders of the demon, who forthwith ran away with him. But Balarâma squeezed and beat him to death, and from this feat gained his name—Râma, "the strong one."[1] Many other demons assumed the forms of savage beasts and met the same fate—Kesin as a wild horse, Byomâsur a wolf, Arishta a bull[2]—all types of the rude animal forms which have attacked mystics and religious men and women since the dawn of religious history. Of another type is the witch Pûtanâ, who tries to suckle the divine child with her devil's milk; but Krishna sucked so hard at her breasts that he drained her life-blood and caused her to perish miserably.[3]

But, beside dragon-slaying, Krishna does many deeds of mercy. He cures the hump-backed woman Kubjâ with a touch; he rescues the son of the Brâhman Sandîpani, who had been slain by the ocean-demon Panchajana. Him Krishna drags from the deep of the sea, and then, like so many divine personages, in the spirit of the Homeric Nekuia, he invades the underworld and rescues the Brâhman boy from the clutches of Yama, god of death, as Herakles saves Alkestis.[4] Another echo of Homeric folklore meets us in his contest with the whirlwind-demon, Trinâvarta, who would have whirled him away; which reminds us of the Thuellai, or wind-gusts, which carry off the daughters of Pandareus, a myth which later on developed into that of the hideous Harpies of Vergil.[5] The event is commemorated at a cell in Mahâban, where

[1] Growse, *loc. cit.*, 59; Wilson-Hall, *loc. cit.*, iv., 300 *seqq.*
[2] Growse, *loc. cit.*, 61, *seqq.*; Wilson-Hall, *loc. cit.*, iv., 333, 340.
[3] Growse, *loc. cit.*, 55; Wilson-Hall, *loc. cit.*, iv., 276.
[4] Growse, *loc. cit.*, 63 *seqq.*
[5] *Iliad*, xvi., 150; *Odyssey*, xx., 66 *seqq.*

the demon-whirlwind is represented by a pair of enormous wings overshadowing the divine child, the same motif which is illustrated on the temple of Apollo at Delos, where Boreas bears away Oreithyia.[1]

Another interesting myth is connected with the rescue of the child by his father Vasu-deva. When he was forced to fly from the tyrant Kamsa, he took Krishna in his arms and plunged with him into the waters of the Jumna, then swollen by the autumn rains. At his first step the water reached the child sleeping in his arms, but as he advanced the wave could rise no higher, and they both crossed in safety. The miracle is commemorated by a brass toy, known as "the Vasu-deva Katora," or the bowl of Vasu-deva, a brass cup enclosing the figure of a man so contrived that when water is poured into it, it cannot rise above the child's foot, being drained away by a hidden duct at the bottom.[2] This same oriental myth is told of the youth Zardusht, who passes over the waste of waters so that the soles of the feet of him and his companions were only moistened.[3] It is thus the eastern version of the tale of St. Christopher, of which there are many representations in the windows of our English churches. Later on the tale was allegorised to represent the Saviour bearing the sins of the world, while in Finnish tradition the saint has been identified with the golden river king, who is invoked to send a host of otters into the net of the hunter.[4] Folklore, in fact, has been busy with this saint, much of whose cult is obviously connected with some primitive worship of a water spirit. Thus, as he waded in the sea, he left his mark on the Dory fish; when he struck his staff into the earth it bloomed and budded, as

[1] Growse, *loc. cit.*, 55; Miss Harrison, *Myths and Monuments of Athens*, Intro., lxvii.

[2] Growse, *loc. cit.*, 54.

[3] Shea-Troyer, *Dabistan*, i., 230.

[4] 1st Series *Notes and Queries*, v., 372 *seqq.*, 495; Abercromby, *Prehistoric Finns*, i., 339; *Gloucestershire Folklore*, 46 *seqq.*

did the Glastonbury thorn and the tooth-pick of the Indian Buddha.[1]

Another remarkable legend is that in which Krishna protects the flocks from rain. The boy, we are told, denied the right of Indra to receive sacrifices, another instance of the conflict of rival cults. The rain-god in his wrath poured down an irresistible deluge, which would have destroyed the flocks had not Krishna raised the hill of Govardhana and shielded them by holding it up on his finger for seven days and nights.[2] The suggestion of Professor Wilson[3] that the story is based on the domed cave or cavern temples in various parts of India hardly explains the matter. We have closer analogues in the Nepalese legends of the peak Tendong, which miraculously elongated itself to save the refugees from the great flood, or the case of the Jaina Saint, Parsva-nâtha, over whom while engaged in his austerities his enemy, Kamatha, caused a mighty rain to fall, on which the Nâga or serpent king, Dharmadhara, shaded him with his hood, a story localised at Ahichhatra in Rohilkhand.[4] We may also compare the many tales of the raising of the sky from the earth, the heaven-pillars, as in the Atlas myth, and stories of the miraculous acts of gods or demons who drop mountains from their aprons as they fly over the earth. St. Anthony of Padua, we are told, was able to keep the rain off his congregation as they prayed in the open air; and the same tale is told of many other saints.[5]

To quote Mr. Growse's summary of another curious legend: "But who so frolicsome as the boy Krishna. Seeing the fair maids of Braj performing their ablutions in the Jumna he stole along the bank, and picking up the

[1] Brand, *Observations*, iii., 194.

[2] Growse, *loc. cit.*, 60; Wilson-Hall, *loc. cit.*, iv., 314 *seqq.*

[3] *Vishnu Purâna*, iv., 316.

[4] Waddell, *Himalayas*, 110; Cunningham, *Ancient Geography of India*, i., 359.

[5] Compare the Australian legend, *Journal of the Anthropological Institute*, vii., 257.

clothes of which they had divested themselves, climbed up with them into a kadamb tree. There he mocked the frightened girls as they came shivering out of the water, nor would he yield a particle of vestment till all had ranged before him in a row, and with clasped and uplifted hands piteously entreated him. Thus the boy taught his votaries that submission to the divine will was a more excellent virtue than even modesty."[1] A most excellent moral drawn from a *risqué* story. Here we have a version of the Swan-maiden cycle of tales which has been so fully discussed by other writers that it is necessary only to refer to it. The tale, I need hardly say, is found in many shapes in Indian folklore.[2]

But the form of the story as it appears in the Krishna cycle is remarkable because it is associated with the Vastra-harana, the sacred tree, which is said to be so named, "the seizing of the clothes," from this incident. Now this appears to be one of the rag-trees so common in all parts of the world, where sick people hang their clothes or fragments of them so as to pass the disease on to the tree-spirit, or to gain strength through communion with the spirit which proves its vitality by reviving with each returning spring. It looks very much as if this may have been the basis of the tale, the clothes hanging on the branches suggesting a further development of the myth in the direction of the Swan-maiden cycle. I am not aware if there are other cases in which the two cycles thus converge. If such be the case it would be interesting as another instance of a not unusual method of the growth of myth.

Passing on from folktales to ritual, we notice, in the first place, that the Krishna cult is very closely associated with

[1] Growse, *loc. cit.*, 59.

[2] *North Indian Notes and Queries*, iii., 120, 153 *seqq.*; Tawney, *loc. cit.*, ii., 453; Miss Stokes, *loc. cit.*, 89; Miss Frere, *Old Deccan Days*, 167 *seqq.* In the *Mahâbhârata, Adi Parva*, sec. 78 (Ray, i., 240), the Gandharva, Chitraratha, mixes up the clothes of the girls while they are bathing.

the observances of the Holî feast, which is nowhere celebrated with more enthusiasm than in places where the worship of Krishna is most popular. Most people are now agreed that these rites of the sacred fire of spring are in the way of a charm to secure the kindly influence of sunshine and the fertility of crops and cattle. If this be so, it supplies another indication that Krishna was originally a local god of agriculture and cattle, with whose cultus such rites would naturally be connected. To this may be added some facts pointing in the same direction. The first is that in India, as in other places, omens are drawn of the prospects of the coming season from the way in which the smoke and blaze of the fire ascend.[1] It was probably from some rural oracle like this that at the temple of the Ismenian Apollo divination was practised by observing the appearance of the sacrificial flame and the ashes of the burnt offerings. In fact, this habit of observing the smoke and fire was reduced to a regular science, known as Pyromanteia or Kapnomanteia.[2]

Another fact from which the same inference may be drawn is the prominence of mock combat and abuse, particularly of women, during the Holî.[3] Customs of this kind are found in many parts of the world. In Greece we have the women's race in honour of Dionysus; the contest of the Spartan boys at the Plane-tree-grove; the raillery directed at women; the yearly contest of maidens with stones and clubs in honour of Athena; the rites of the Dædala; the sham fight at the Eleusinia; the Lithobolia or stone-throwing custom at Troezen; the Taurokalapsia or Thessalian bull-fight, and so on.[4] In Rome the same

[1] Crooke, *Agricultural and Rural Glossary*, 125.

[2] Sophocles, *Œd. Rex*, 21; *Antig.*, 1005 *seqq.*; Herodotus, viii., 134; Euripides, *Phœn.*, 1285 *seqq.*; Frazer, *Golden Bough*, ii., 270; Smith, *Dictionary of Antiquities* (2nd ed.), i., 646.

[3] Growse, *loc. cit.*, 92; Crooke, *Popular Religion*, ii., 316.

[4] Pausanias, iii., 13, 7; ix., 32, 2; Frazer, *Golden Bough*, i., 91 *seqq.*; Frazer, *Pausanias*, ii., 492; iii., 267 *seqq.*; Herodotus, iv., 180.

custom is represented by the Equirria or Mamuralia, the Matronalia Festa, the Liberalia and the Lupercalia, in which there was a mock human sacrifice, the foreheads of the youths being smeared with the knives still dripping from the slaughter of the victims.[1] This, we know, was a common charm to promote the fertility of the crops, and a survival of rites like these may possibly be traced in the modern carnival.

In India we have many instances of the same type—the Bagwah or stone-throwing in Kumaun; the Barra, or tug of war between adjoining villages, which is part of the funeral rites of the Maghs; the combat between the people of the two quarters of the town of Pushkar; the sham fights in the Hindu Kush, where women are privileged to abuse the Ra or chief; the stone-throwing rite at Ahmadnagar, which if discontinued causes a plague of rats, if well done brings abundant rain; and among the Bhîls a branch of a tree is planted in the ground which the men try to uproot and are belaboured by women.[2]

Going further afield, we have the scramble to ascend a tree among the Nahuas of Western America; the flinging of cocoanuts as a rain charm in Ceylon; the Dayak combat to scare evil spirits; the stoning custom at Seoul in Corea; the Kâfirs of the Hindu Kush flinging an iron ball on a holiday or fighting with snowballs at the Taska feast; the Burmese women at the new year flinging water over each other; the abuse of women and unrestrained sexual licence at the Nanga rites in Fiji, which may be a survival of group-marriage, now invested with a ritual significance; the flinging of stones at the doors of the cells occupied by holy men

[1] Smith, *loc. cit.*, i., 753.

[2] Crooke, *loc. cit.*, ii., 321; *North Indian Notes and Queries*, iii., 99; Risley, *Tribes and Castes*, ii., 34; Broughton, *Letters from a Mahratta Camp*, 356 *seqq.* And compare Frazer, *Pausanias*, ii., 492; iii., 267; *Indian Antiquary*, v., 5; vi., 29.

at the Phapa rites in Siam; and the mock combats of various American Indian tribes.[1]

I need hardly refer to the cases of the late survivals of tribal contests in Great Britain which have been illustrated by Mr. G. L. Gomme.[2] We know that many of the most ancient fairs in this country are connected with the ancient cemeteries and some cult of the dead in which mock combats and even blood-letting were part of the observances. It would be tempting to suggest that we have a similar ritual survival in some of our English games, like "The Raid," "Scotch and English," and "Prisoners' Base."[3] Bull-baiting, again, which in some cases seems to be a survival of a water-sacrifice,[4] often takes the form of a contest between rival villages or townships. Akin to these are other popular ceremonials in which animals take part, such as the habit of horse-riding at certain feasts.[5] Wren-hunting, which is done by fishermen in the Isle of Man to keep off storms, was originally possibly a procession in honour of the sacred beast which later on turned into a hunt, like the custom of the Munda girls in India, who on a feast-day hunt and kill any pigs, sheep, or goats of neighbouring villages which they can come across, and that of the youths in Bihâr, who have a festival on which they hunt hares and jackals.[6]

[1] Bancroft, *loc. cit.*, ii., 330; i., 84; *Panjab Notes and Queries*, iii., 85; Ling Roth, *loc. cit.*, i., 260, 414; *The Times*, 8th September, 1891; Robertson, *Kâfirs of the Hindu Kush*, 584 *seqq.*, 592; Symes, *Mission to the Court of Awa*, ii., 210; *Burmah Gazetteer*, i., 417; *Reports, American Bureau of Ethnology*, 1881-82, 295, 337; Jarves, *History of the Hawaiian or Sandwich Islands*, 153; Bowring, *Siam*, i., 159 *seqq; Journal of the Anthropological Institute*, xxi., 126.

[2] *Village Communities*, 240.

[3] Mrs. Gomme, *Traditional Games*, ii., 79 *seqq.*, 183; *Denham Tracts*, i., 151 *seqq.*

[4] *Folk-Lore*, vii., 346.

[5] Martin in Pinkerton, *Travels*, iii., 600, 606, 668, 716.

[6] Frazer, *Golden Bough*, ii., 140; Bancroft, *loc. cit.*, ii., 336; *Denham Tracts*, i., 203; *North Indian Notes and Queries*, iii., 98; Grierson, *Bihâr Peasant Life*, 401; Gomme, *loc. cit.*, 112 *seqq.*; *Folk-Lore*, iii., 463 *seqq.*

The same idea may underlie some of our most popular village rites in this country—the Hood Game at Haxey;[1] the ball contests at Bury St. Edmunds and Newcastle;[2] the ram-hunting at Eton;[3] the bull-baiting at Stamford and Great Grimsby;[4] the ball playing on Shrove Tuesday at Whitby, where if the game be not well played the youngsters will be sure to fall ill at harvest time; similar rites at St. Ives, Dorking and Nuneaton; the Whipping Toms at Leicester; the whipping of the cat in Shropshire; the catching of a hare at Cleshill in Warwickshire; and the hurling of pitchers into houses in Cornwall.[5] A closer parallel to the Hindu rite may be found in the custom of mock-combat round a bonfire at Marlborough on the 5th of November.[6]

The published accounts of many of these rites are very meagre; but we may perhaps see in some or all of them one of two principles—either a racial or tribal contest between the residents of adjoining villages or parts of the same township—or survivals of some form of animal or perhaps human sacrifice, the object being to propitiate the powers of evil which affect the fertility of the crops or injure children or cattle.

Another important rite connected with Kris̆hna worship is that of swinging the idol or one of the devotees before the image of the god. In Bengal this rite is known as the Dola Yâtra or swinging rite, and is performed in spring or

[1] *Folk-Lore*, vii., 330 *seqq.*; 2nd Series *Notes and Queries*, iv., 486; 4th series, ix., 158 *seqq.*

[2] Hone, *Everyday Book* (ed. 1878), i., 215.

[3] 7th Series *Notes and Queries*, iv., 416, 467; 2nd Series, vii., 201.

[4] 5th Series *Notes and Queries*, ii., 224; Hone, *loc. cit.*, i., 741; *Gentleman's Magazine Library*, *Manners and Customs*, 211 *seqq.*

[5] 5th Series *Notes and Queries*, vii., 120; 8th Series, viii., 28; 1st Series, ix., 223 *seqq.*; 3rd Series, i., 224; 6th Series, i., 154; 1st Series, vii., 235; 2nd Series, vii., 312; Hone, *Year Book* (ed. 1878), 269; *Gentleman's Magazine, loc. cit.*, 258.

[6] 1st Series *Notes and Queries*, v., 365.

about the middle of March. The image of the god is carried on a swing or placed in a seat or cradle, which as soon as the dawn appears is set quietly in motion for a few turns. This is repeated at noon and again at sunset. During the day, as at the Holî in Northern India, a good deal of horseplay goes on, sprinkling of coloured powder and water, abuse of women, and so on.[1] In Northern India, at the Tîj or third day of the month Sâvan, in the autumn is a woman's feast, when they bathe, dress in their best, and swing in merry-go-rounds.[2] In the month of Sâvan in Bengal, Dharmarâja, who is here probably identified with Yama, god of death, has a feast where swinging goes on.[3] The rite of swinging Krishna is also performed at Jaggannâth, and Mr. Pegge gives an illustration and account of the rite, while in Bombay a special fair of the same kind is held at Yellama's Hill.[4] The Bengal hook-swinging rite, at which devotees torture themselves and some swing with hooks passed through the loins, has been often described. It prevailed in many parts of the country, and instances have been reported in quite recent times. The swinging of the god Lingo is prominent in the Gond Epic, and the swinging of witches is still common among some of the jungle tribes.[5]

These swinging rites prevail in many parts of the world. In Greece we have the Aiora, which is based on a legend that Dionysus was received by Icarius and taught the culture of the vine. Icarius gave some of the wine to the neighbouring peasants, who believed that they had been poisoned by it, and slew him. When they came to their senses they buried him, and his daughter, Erigone, guided to the grave

[1] Wilson, *Essays*, ii., 224 *seqq.*; Ward, *Hindoos*, ii., 171; Monier Williams, *Hinduism and Brâhmanism*, 430.

[2] *North Indian Notes and Queries*, iv., 149.

[3] *Ibid.*, i., 76.

[4] Pegge, *Orissa Mission*, 118 *seqq.*; *Bombay Gazetteer*, xxi., 613.

[5] Hislop, *Aboriginal Tribes*, App. 28; compare Ling Roth, *loc. cit.*, i., 368.

by her favourite dog, Maera, hanged herself on a tree close by. Dionysus thereupon sent a grievous plague which could be stayed only by the offering to him of the Phallus. Then, in order to appease the ghost of Erigone, the Athenian maidens all began to hang themselves. This madness could be appeased only by the institution of the feast of the Aiora, in which maidens swing themselves on trees, a clear instance of a folktale invented to explain a piece of primitive ritual.[1] By another story the rite seems to have been connected with the suicide of Phædra.[2] The Aiora has come down to modern times in the Greek islands. "On the Tuesday after Easter the maidens of Seriphos play their favourite game of the swing. They hang a rope from one wall to the other, put some clothes on it, and swing, singing and swinging one after another. Aware of this, the young men try to pass by, and are called upon for a toll of one penny each, a song, and a swing. The words they use are as follows: 'The gold is swung, the silver is swung, and swung, too, is my love with the golden hair.' To which the maiden replies: 'Who is it that swings me that I may gild him with my favour, that I may work him a fez all covered with pearls?' Then, having paid his penny, he is permitted to pass, and another comes and does likewise." [3]

The origin of these rites is obscure. In some cases they seem to represent merely a fertility charm, as when in Madras the Reddi brings home his bride, a swing is hung from the house-beam, a wooden doll is hung in it, and swung by husband and wife, while the women sing songs, obviously a charm to make their union fertile.[4] In other cases it may be connected with the rule which prevents divine personages and those under taboo, as girls when

[1] Miss Harrison, *loc. cit.*, Intro., xxxix.; Frazer, *Pausanias*, ii., 461; *Classical Review*, iii., 378 *seqq*.

[2] Pausanias, x., 29, 3.

[3] Bent, *Cyclades*, 5.

[4] *Bombay Gazetteer*, xviii. (1), 405.

they come of age, from touching either heaven or earth.[1] We have, again, the common custom of hanging masks on trees, which swing about and are supposed to promote their fertility—the Oscilla of Rome and the Dozzils of parts of England.[2] A bull-roarer is swung in the same way in the neighbourhood of Torres Straits as a fishing charm, and in Celebes dolls are hung on trees to protect the fruit.[3] In the same class is probably the cult of Aparchomeme, the "hanging" Artemis. The children, we are told, hung up images of Artemis, and the men of Kaphyæ stoned them. The angry goddess smote their wives with sore disease, and thus the cult of the Hanging Artemis came to be instituted. We find also the same idea in the worship of Helene Dendritis.[4]

It shows itself in India in the custom of hanging up little cots on trees as a remedy for disease. In Madras when cholera appears, a swing is put up in the shrine of Bhangarmâ and worshipped.[5] In fact, the idea seems to have generally prevailed that the swinging of anything before a god, from the hook-swinging of a devotee to the whirling Dervishes, was a mode of propitiating the divinity, every part of the person or thing offered being brought in succession into the immediate view of the god. Thus, we have in India the Evil Eye protectives of swinging lamps, rice pounders, and what not, round the head of the married pair. The Nahuas of Western America swung censers before their images and before the sun,[6] and the swinging censer has come down to the Christianity of our own days. It is no doubt in consonance with some ancient rite of propitia-

[1] Frazer, *Golden Bough*, i., 223 *seqq.*

[2] Vergil, *Georgics*, i., 382 *seqq.*; Smith, *Dictionary of Antiquities*, ii., 305; *Folklore*, vii., 399.

[3] *Journal of the Anthropological Institute*, xix., 406.

[4] Farnell, *Cults of the Greek States*, ii., 428, 634; Pausanias, vi., 22, 5.

[5] Crooke, *loc. cit.*, i., 97; Oppert, *Original Inhabitants of Bharutavarsha*, 154.

[6] Bancroft, *loc. cit.*, ii., 318.

tion that in Bolivia people swing all day long on All Souls' Day in the hope that while they swing they may approach the spirits of their departed friends as they fly from Purgatory to Paradise. They swing as high as they can, so as to reach the topmost branches of the trees, and whenever they are able to pull off one of the higher boughs they think that they release a soul from Purgatory.[1]

A large part of the Krishna legend relates to his amours with the Gopis, the wives and daughters of the herdsmen of the land of Braj. On this is based many of the erotic myths which form such a repulsive element in modern Vaishnavism. "Drawn from their lonely homes," as Mr. Growse tells the story,[2] "by the low sweet notes of his seductive pipe, they floated round him in rapturous love, and through the moonlight autumn nights joined him in the circling dance, passing from glade to glade in ever-increasing ecstacy of passion. To whatever theme his voice was attuned, their song had but one burden—his perfect beauty; and as they mingled in the mystic maze, with eyes closed in the intensity of voluptuous passion, each nymph as she grasped the hand of her partner thrilled at the touch, as though the hand were Krishna's, and dreamed herself alone supremely blessed in his undivided affection. Râdhâ, fairest of the fair, reigned queen of the revels, and so languished in the heavenly delights of his embraces that all consciousness of earth and self was obliterated."

This is the dance known as the Râsa-mandala, or circular dance, and in the popular representations of it "whatever the number of Gopis introduced so often is the figure of Krishna repeated. Thus each Gopi can claim him as a partner, while again in the centre of the circle he stands in larger form with his favourite, Râdhâ." By a similar legend a friend challenged Krishna to bestow on

[1] 8th Series *Notes and Queries*, vi., 345.

[2] Growse, *loc. cit.*, 61.

him one of his wives. "In whatever room thou findest me not," he answered, "she is thine;" and Saubhari the sage, we are told, visited all the daughters of King Mandhatri at the same time.[1]

This is not the place to discuss the question of religious dances at any length. This much seems fairly clear, that they are often intended to act as a charm to promote the fertility of the animal and vegetable world. Pausanias tells us that one part of the cult of the chthonic powers, among whom the vegetation deities hold a prominent place, was the smiting of the underground folk with rods; and to this day at their seasonal dances the Kol girls in India kneel and pat the ground in time to the music, as if coaxing it to be productive.[2] The dance, then, was apparently a variant of this, and the beating of the ground by the feet of the dancers was an attempt to wake the slumbering gods of growth at each recurring spring. When, as in the Râsa-mandala, the dance took a circular form, another kind of charm was added, of which the tale of instances is legion.

We may, then, in the first place, compare with this dance of Krishna and the women that of the Grecian nymphs, the spirits of wood and spring, through whom the earth gives its increase. Homer tells us that they have fair dancing grounds and dance round Achelous, while the Agronomoi or wild-wood nymphs disport themselves with Artemis.[3] Their successors, the modern fairies, dance in the "Midsummer Night's Dream," and rustics sometimes are privileged to see their dances in the England and Germany of our days.[4] Like these are the dances of the Maenads, that

[1] Shea-Troyer, *Dabistan*, iii., 32; Wilson-Hall, *loc. cit.*, iii., 274.

[2] Pausanias, viii., 15, 3, with Frazer's note; *Journal of the Asiatic Society of Bengal*, xxxv. (2), 184.

[3] *Odyssey*, vi., 105: xii., 318; *Iliad*, xxiv., 615 *seqq.*

[4] Aubrey, *Remaines*, 28; Grimm, *loc. cit.*, ii., 555; *Folk-Lore Record*, i., 27; Jones-Kropf, *Magyar Folk-Tales*, Intro., xxxiv.

of the naked youths in honour of Apollo, that of the Lacedaemonian maidens, and that of the Thyiads in Athens, the rite of Mother Dindymene and the Kordax on Mount Sipylus.[1] It is repeated in that of the Salii at Rome, and in the ritual of the Floralia. Of modern instances it is only necessary to name the puberty- and wedding-dance among savages, the Zulus for instance, and to this day there is a special wedding-dance in Brittany.[2] It is doubtless with the same motive that the Madonna del Mateno of Sardinia pirouettes in public, that there is a Whitsuntide dance at Echternach in Luxemburgh, and that the Mexicans dance in honour of Our Lady of Guadalupe.[3] We have another survival of the same rite in the Furry or Faddy dance at Helston in Cornwall, which is said to commemorate a dragon which once passed over the town without doing any harm, possibly a reminiscence of the great rain-serpent.[4]

Secondly, in the Gopis we may recognise the temple-slaves of the East, concubines of the god, known in India as Devi-dâsis, an institution connected with the custom of marriage to the god, of which I have given many instances in another place.[5] The same custom prevailed in Egypt; and these divine dancers passed into the Greek world as the Hierodouloi, of whom Strabo tells us there were six

[1] Pausanias, iii., 11, 9; 10, 7; iv., 16, 9; x., 4, 3; vi., 22, 1; Frazer, ii., 411; iii., 320; iv., 95, 147.

[2] Theal, *loc. cit.*, 217; 8th Series *Notes and Queries*, vi., 481; Frazer, *Pausanias*, iii., 469.

[3] 8th Series *Notes and Queries*, x., 397; 7th Series, ix., 381; 8th Series, x., 115, 202,

[4] 6th Series *Notes and Queries*, xi., 468, 496; 5th Series, v., 507; vi., 32; 7th Series, ix., 424; Hone, *Everyday Book*, ii.. 324 *seqq.*; *Gentleman's Magazine*, *loc. cit.*, 216 *seqq.*

[5] *North Indian Notes and Queries*, iv., 9 *seqq.*; C. Ramachendrier, *Collection of Decisions of the High Court and Privy Council on Dancing Girls*, Intro., 1 *seqq.*; Crooke, *loc. cit.*, ii., 118; *Bombay Gazetteer*, xviii. (1), 546; Dubois, *Hindu Manners, Customs, and Ceremonies*, (ed. Beauchamp) 133, 592; Yule, *Marco Polo*, ii., 288 *seqq.*

thousand at the temple of the Cappadocian Comana and three thousand at Morimene, while the early Musalmân invaders found five hundred at the great temple of Somnâth.[1] A variant of this institution leads us to the fable of the Amazons and the Land of Women of Celtic legend.[2]

I have left to the end of this Paper what is perhaps the most interesting part of the Krishna myths, the explanation of his name. The word means, "the black, the dark, or the dark blue one," and in the popular representations of him he is usually depicted as of a dark blue hue. The popular Hindu explanation, that he was originally born black, does not help us to an explanation. The difficulty of explaining his name was felt at a very early time, as is shown by the attempt to derive it from *krishi*, "ploughing," or from *krishi*, "what existeth," and *na*, "eternal peace."[3] He may be, as we have seen, an agricultural god, but his name cannot be derived from his functions. Equally inconclusive is the view of one school of comparative mythologists, which identifies him with the setting sun.

His title opens up a very curious chapter in religious symbolism, that of the black or otherwise coloured gods.

To begin with Egypt, we have black gods in Isis and Osiris, the latter in his form as god of the dead, while he is green when a corn-god.[4] Ammon is a blue god, which is the colour of the modern Buddhist ghosts, while Krishna is one of the nine black Vasu-devas of the Jainas, and by the early Buddhists he was regarded as the chief of the black

[1] Herodotus, i., 199; Maspero, *Dawn of Civilisation*, 126, 676; *Struggle of the Nations*, 161, 182; Müller, *Dorians*, i., 282 *seqq.*; Frazer, *Pausanias*, iii., 30, 450; Smith, *Dictionary of Antiquities* (2nd ed.), i., 959; *Encyclopædia Biblica*, i., 338.

[2] Nutt, *Voyage of Bran*, i., 30, 146.

[3] Muir, *loc. cit.*, iv., 219; *Mahâbhârata*, *Udyoga Parva*, sec. 69, Ray trans., iii., 227.

[4] Plutarch, *De Iside*, 33; Wilkinson, *Ancient Egyptians* (ed. 1878), iii., 81; Maspero, *Dawn of Civilisation*, 73; Erman, *Life in Ancient Egypt*, 305; Frazer, *Golden Bough*, i., 403.

demons.[1] In Egypt Hâpi, the Nile god, is sometimes red and sometimes blue.[2]

In Mexico, Acosta describes the idol of Vitziliputzli: "It was an image of wood like to a man, set upon a stoole of the colour of Azure, in a brancard or litter, at every corner was a piece of wood in form of a serpent's head. The stoole signified that he was set in heaven; the idoll had all the forehead azure, and had a band of azure under the nose from one ear to another."[3] The aspect of other Mexican gods was similar, as that of Chalchihuitlicue and Cipattonal.[4] Blue seems to have been a sacred colour, as in Yucatan the assistants of sorcerers painted themselves blue, which was the colour of the books used by the priests and at special feasts of the gods, the instruments used in every profession, the doors of houses, and even children were daubed with blue.[5]

In India black gods abound. Besides those to whom statues of black stone are dedicated, of which more later on, we have Siva and Râhu, Vishnu, Târâ, and Kâlî-devî. Siva, again, is known as Nîla-kantha, or "blue-necked," to explain which a myth was invented that his colour was derived from the drinking of the deadly poison, which otherwise would have destroyed the world. Sâraswatî, a river goddess, is blue; and in his form as Nârâyana Vishnu has a blue stone image in Nepâl.[6] The colour of Nârâyana obviously attracted attention in early times, for we have in the Mahâbhârata a story that it was only in the Iron Age that he became black.[7]

Among other black gods may be named the Japanese Dai

[1] Bunsen, *Egypt's Place*, i., 370.

[2] Maspero, *loc. cit.*, 37.

[3] Bancroft, *loc. cit.*, iii., 291.

[4] *Ibid.*, iii., 297, 368, 491.

[5] *Ibid.*, ii., 697, 700.

[6] Growse, *Râmâyana of Tulsi Dâs*, 49; Ward, *Hindoos*, ii., 26, 147; *Asiatic Researches*, ii., 313.

[7] *Mahâbhârata, Vana Parva*, sec. 149; Ray, trans., ii., 448.

Gakf, "the great black one," who is a god of riches, like the Hindu Kuvera, "the ugly one," both probably black spirits of the hearth, like Brownie and the Cauld Lad of Hilton.[1] Malignant spirits and ghosts are naturally depicted as black, such as the cruel wood-sprite in Terra del Fuego, and the Ukraine god of evil. Our own Devil and others of his kinsfolk are described as black, and Pausanias speaks of the black ghost of Temesa.[2]

Passing on to Greece, we have the Nocturnal Dionysus and Dionysus of the Black Goatskin, the Black Erinys, the Black Aphrodite, said to be so called because men indulge in vice at night, but who was really a chthonic deity of the grave, and the Black Demeter.[3]

English tradition supplies us with a black Godiva, who is doubtless a decayed deity of the older paganism.[4]

In more modern times we have the host of Black Madonnas, a very curious chapter in the history of hagiology.[5] The legends given in explanation of their colour are of many kinds. Thus the image of Maria Egyptiaca was entirely covered with hair to represent her dwelling in the desert, "al black over all her body of the grate heat and brennynge of the sun," as the Golden Legend describes her.[6] Others are said to have been buried in the earth or bogs,

[1] Gomme, *Folklore Relics of Village Life*, 88; the Mexican Yxtliton or Ixthilton, "the little negro," or "the black-faced," cured children of various diseases. Bancroft, *loc. cit.*, iii., 409.

[2] *Journal of the Anthropological Institute*, x. 40; xii., 158, 162; xv., 145; Ralston, *Russian Fairy Tales*, 358; Pausanias, vi., 6, 11; Frazer, iv., 357.

[3] Pausanias, i., 40, 6; ii., 35, 1; Frazer, ii., 525 *seqq.*; Aeschylus, *Choeph*, 1038; *Sept. Contra Thebes*, 696, 975; Euripides, *Orestes*, 321; *Electra*, 1345; Pausanias, viii., 34, 3; ii., 2, 4; viii., 6, 5; ix., 27, 5; Farnell, *loc. cit.*, ii., 649 *seqq.*; Pausanias, viii., 5, 8, 42, 1; Frazer, iv., 406.

[4] Hartland, *Science of Fairy Tales*, 85.

[5] Grimm, *loc. cit.*, i., 313; Inman, *Ancient Faiths*, ii., 263; Brewer, *Dictionary of Miracles*, 526; 9th Series *Notes and Queries*, ii., 367, 397, 449, 475, 537; iii., 190, 376 *seqq.*, 452; iv., 77, 135, 177, 315.

[6] Fosbroke, *Cyclopædia of Antiquities*, i., 102, quoting *Golden Legend*, fol. lxxii.

and to have been recovered from thence by some favoured votary. Such is the famous Madonna la Trouche, that found in the Cullen bog near Tipperary, the Madonna of Ballyvourney in the county of Cork, and that of St. Molaise at Innismurray.[1]

Blackness is the characteristic of images other than Madonnas, such as the rag images of the Italian Befanas, which take the place of our Santa Claus and have blackened faces.[2]

The question of the explanation of the origin of these black gods is extremely complex.

In some cases we may suspect that they represent a racial type familiar to the people who first introduced this form of worship. We must remember that among some races blackness of complexion is not alone considered not unbecoming, but is even admired. One of the titles of the Zulu kings, for instance, was "You who are black;" and the lady in the Canticles says, "I am black but comely, O daughters of Jerusalem."[3] We find the Egyptian queen, Nofritari, consort of Ahmosis, identified with Isis and depicted as a black-skinned goddess.[4] Hence we can explain why St. Benedito, a black negro saint is worshipped on the Amazon, and on the Gold Coast the white man's God is said to be black, and he appears at the foot of the fetish-tree in the form of a black dog.[5]

Now it has been often noticed that some of the forms of the Indian Buddha and other black Hindu gods are of a distinctively negroid type, representing the deity with thick lips, long hanging ear lobes, and black curly hair

[1] Rhys, *Hibbert Lectures*, 102; O'Curry, *Manners and Customs*, iii., 206 *note*; Borlase, *Dolmens of Ireland*, iii., 788, 1115; Southey, *Commonplace Book*, iii., 174.

[2] 6th Series *Notes and Queries*, ii., 409.

[3] Darwin, *Descent of Man*, 579; *Canticles*, i., 5; *Journal of the Anthropological Institute*, xv., 56; Featherman, *Negritoes*, 584 *note*.

[4] Maspero, *Struggle of the Nations*, 96, 98.

[5] Bates, *Amazon*, i., 310 *seqq.*; Featherman, *loc. cit.*, 160 *note*.

which cannot be referred to any existing Indian people.[1] Dr. Waddell describes the Lama of Tibet as a man with short curly hair, like the conventional images of Buddha; the courtiers depicted in the rock paintings of the Ajanta caves have fair or dark brown curly hair, while the attendants are black with curly negroid hair, and some are dwarfs; the images of the Jaina saint Gautama have crisp curly hair, thick lips, and black skin.[2] The enlargement of the ear lobe has also been often noticed.[3] Mr. Walhouse thus describes the image of Buddha at Karakal in South Kanara:[4] "Remarkable it is, too, that the features show nothing distinctively Hindu. The hair grows in close crisp curls; the broad fleshy cheeks might make the face seem heavy, were it not for the marked and dignified expression conferred by the calm forward gazing eyes and aquiline nose, somewhat pointed at tip. The forehead is of average size, the lips very full and thick, the upper one long almost to ugliness, throwing the chin, though full and prominent, into the shade. The arms, which touch the body only at the hips, are remarkably long, the large, well-formed hands and fingers reaching to the knees." It may be suspected that in these representations we have a proof of negroid or negrito influence on Indian religious beliefs.

Again, in some cases, the blackness of certain images serves only to connote extreme antiquity. As we have seen, some of them are said to have been found in bogs or buried in the ground, and their dark appearance would corroborate this view of their origin, and sometimes, perhaps, tend to the growth of a conventional type. We know that in the Roman Catholic and Eastern churches it is a common

[1] *Bombay Gazetteer*, xiv., 83; *Gujarat Gazetteer*, i., 458 *note; Asiatic Researches*, iii., 122.

[2] Waddell, *Among the Himalayas*, 161; *Bombay Gazetteer*, xii., 488; xiv., 67; xv. (1), 232.

[3] *Journal of the Anthropological Institute*, ii., 192 *seqq.*

[4] *Frazer's Magazine*, May, 1875.

incident in the ritual to burn candles or incense before such images; and an ancient Madonna would naturally become darkened in this way, as the fetish stone in an Indian village becomes dark from repeated oblations of oil and butter. The famous Black Rood of Scotland, for instance, seems to have presented the appearance of being blackened all over.[1] It was possibly the natural reverence felt towards old blackened images which suggested to the Greeks the construction of so many of their Xoana from ebony.[2]

In the same way, too, many of these images are said to have been blackened by fire. Thus we have the image of the Ithomatian Zeus, which was said to have been found in a burned forest, and there was another charred image of Athena.[3] So Fryer describes a pagoda at Gokarna in Kanara made of black marble, and particularly venerated because it had escaped the fire.[4] The same tale is told of a Lingam at Mândhâta in the Central Provinces.[5] Al Azraki tells us that the black stone of Mecca was once of a refulgent bright colour, but became repeatedly blackened by fire both before and after the rise of Islâm.[6] We have a similar instance in the image of the rough black stone which represents the jungle goddess Porâ Mâî, which is said to have been rescued from a burning forest.[7]

At any rate the worship of black stones is a well-marked phase in the history of early religion. Among these we have the Bætuli of Syria, a word which is another form of the better known Hebrew Bethel.[8] One of the Fiji gods is

[1] 1st Series *Notes and Queries*, ii., 409.

[2] Pausanias, i., 35, 3; 42, 5; ii., 22, 5; viii., 17, 2; 53, 11.

[3] *Ibid.*, iii., 26, 6; i., 27, 6.

[4] *East India and Persia*, 159 *seqq.*

[5] *Central Provinces Gazetteer*, 261.

[6] Burckhardt, *Travels*, i., 297.

[7] Crooke, *loc. cit.*, i., 114 *seqq.* The same story is told of the Santo Nino de Cebú and of a famous Cross in the Philippine Islands. Foreman, *Philippine Islands* (2nd ed.), 196 *seqq.*

[8] Pliny, *Nat. Hist.*, xxxvii., 135; *Encyclopædia Biblica*, 569 *note.*

a black milestone, and in Bengal, Ward informs us, all stone images are of black marble, and the same type is particularly common in Bombay.[1] We may add the Sâla-grâma, or black ammonite, which represents Vishnu, and in Guatemala the famous oracular stone of Patinamit is black.[2]

We may suspect that many of these sacred black stones may have been originally meteorites.[3] It is not difficult to understand why the sudden fall of a stone from the sky, the fall being often accompanied by terrifying sounds, or the train of fire flung behind it by a "falling star," should cause extreme terror to the beholders, and excite awe and reverence. We find in many places traditions of what the Greek called a Diopetes Agalma, which our authorised version of the Acts of the Apostles calls "the image which fell down from Jupiter."[4] This was the famous image of Diana of Ephesus, of which we know little, save that it was black. Some say that it was a stone, others that it was made of ebony or vine wood, and had never been changed though the temple had been seven times rebuilt.[5] Other Greek images were said to have fallen from heaven, like the Athena of the Akropolis, the Artemis of Taurus, the Sicilian Demeter, the Aphrodite of Paphos, and the Cybele of Pessinus. In the same way Elegabalus in Sun-form was worshipped at Emesa in the shape of a black conical stone,

[1] Williams, *Fiji*, i., 221; Ward, *Hindoos*, ii., 233; *Asiatic Researches*, v., 240 *note*; iv., 46, 48; xi., 535; Atkinson, *Himalayan Gazetteer*, iii., 24; *Bombay Gazetteer*, xvi., 517; xix., 450, 486, 530, 546, 582, 611; xx., 438, 442, 448, 450, 452, 455, 459, 465, 467; xxi., 521; xxii., 714, 807; xxiii., 550, 552, 679; xxiv., 300, 377; *Journal of tha Asiatic Society, Bengal*, xxxiii., 209.

[2] Bancroft, *loc. cit.*, iv. 123.

[3] On this see the paper by Professor H. A. Miers, F.R.S., read at the 1898 meeting of the British Association, from which I have taken several of the following instances.

[4] Acts, xix., 35.

[5] Pliny, *Nat. Hist.*, xvi., 79; Farrar, *St. Paul*, 358; *Encyclopædia Biblica*, i., 1099.

which was reported to have fallen from the sky.[1] In Mexico, Quetzalcoatl was represented by a black stone or by several small green stones, most likely aerolites which were said to have fallen from heaven.[2] In India the image of Vasu-deva, father of Krishna, came down from the heaven of Indra, thus connecting Krishna with an aerolite cult; that of Sîtalâ at Jasoli fell from the sky, and the ancestors of the Madaga sept of Kâfirs in the Hindu Kush, and that of the Mech in Assam came down from the sky in a thunderbolt, as the stone which Kronos spewed up was worshipped, and the Syrian Aphrodite sprang from an egg which fell from heaven into the Euphrates.[3]

As might naturally be expected the worship of aerolites is widespread. Many races call flint weapons "thunderbolts"; healing powers are attributed to them; they are hung over cattle sheds and round the necks of children; they are worshipped by the Khyens of Assam; one was found in South Russia, set in a gold ring, and was no doubt used as an amulet.[4] So, stone knives, following the potent influence of conservatism in religious matters, were largely used in ritual, in slaying swine in Rome, in Egyptian embalmment, in the Hebrew rite of circumcision.[5]

The number of sacred meteorites is legion. Professor Miers mentions one that fell in Ensisheim in Elsass in 1492, which was taken to the village church, where it is still preserved. An aerolite fell in Sugolia on the borders of Hungary

[1] Gibbon, *Decline and Fall* (ed. W. Smith), i., 281.

[2] Bancroft, *loc. cit.*, iii., 281.

[3] Atkinson, *Himalayan Gazetteer*, ii., 785, 800; Robertson, *Kâfirs of the Hindu Kush*, 160 *seqq.*; Pausanias, x., 24, 6; Frazer, iii., 339; Risley, *Tribes and Castes of Bengal*, ii., 87.

[4] Frazer, *Pausanias*, v., 355; 8th Series *Notes and Queries*, ii., 321; Tylor, *Early History*, 208; Grimm, *loc. cit.*, iv., 1221, 1686; Dalyell, *Darker Superstitions of Scotland*, 356 *seqq.*; *Journal of the Anthropological Institute*, i., App., lxii.; vi., 149.

[5] Livy, i., 24; Herodotus, ii., 86; *Exodus*, iv. 25.

in 1514, which was hung in a church on an iron chain.[1] Raffles speaks of one which fell in Java in 1421, which is preserved as a sacred object in a mosque. One at Charcas in Mexico is built into the wall of a church and worshipped by women. Another, which fell at Benares in 1798, was supposed to imply the anger of the gods; and another, seen in Râjputâna in 1867, was promptly ground to powder by the people to render it harmless. At the tomb of Mahmûd in Bijapur is what is called a meteoric stone hanging from a chain which is said to guard the tomb from lightning: it is really a piece of nephrite or jade.[2] Mr. Walhouse describes a similar stone in Southern India.[3] In 1802 one fell at l'Aigle in France, which from the fright it caused is said to have effected the conversion of a sceptic. After the fall of one in Ardèche the peasants would not work near the spot till they had sprinkled it with holy water. In East Africa, in 1853, such a stone was anointed with oil, dressed with beads and set up as a god. An Indian stone was "decked with flowers, daily anointed with *ghi*, or clarified butter, and subjected to frequent ceremonial worship and coatings of sandal-wood powder." Two which fell in Japan more than one hundred and fifty years ago were formerly worshipped yearly at the temple in Ogi. One of them is now in the British Museum, where any member of the Society so disposed may start a local cult of his own. As I write, I find in *The Times*[4] an account of a stone which fell at Mount Zomba in British East Africa in January last. The people sat round it thinking it miraculous and enchanted.

Finally may be mentioned the well-known meteorite of Aigospotami, the Hajar-ul-Aswad, or great black stone, at the Kaaba in Mecca, which is clearly an aerolite, and that

[1] 7th Series *Notes and Queries*, vi., 325.

[2] *Bombay Gazetteer*, xxiii., 606.

[3] *Journal of the Anthropological Institute*, vii., 35 *seqq.*

[4] 18 May, 1899; other Indian examples in *Bombay Gazetteer*, xv. (2), 275; *Journal of the Asiatic Society, Bengal*, xxx., 415.

worshipped at Sîtamarhi in Bengal under the title of Adbhûtnâtha, or "the miraculous god."[1]

We are then, perhaps, justified in suspecting that more than one line of influence may have contributed to the representation of Krishna as a black god.

There is, first, the Negrito element, which shows itself in the popular representations of Buddha.

Secondly, if Krishna in his earliest form be a god of agriculture and cattle, the blackness may connote his chthonic attributes.

Thirdly, if the Râjputs may be identified with the Yu-echi of Central Asia, they may have brought their black god with them. In this part of the world to this day black gods are found. At Tashkent is the shrine of the saint Zangata, "the dark father," who is said to have been dark like a negro; and a black stone near Bukhâra, called Sianghi Murâd, is rubbed by pilgrims, who touch their faces and beards with it.[2] There is also much in the earlier legends of the Râjputs which suggests an influence which, whatever it may have been, was probably not Hindu. The Pândavas were probably a rude non-Aryan confederation and brought with them foreign practices, such as polyandry, which shows itself in the Draupadi Legend, brutality to conquered enemies, as when Bhima drains the life-blood of Duscâsana.[3] The brutal practices of Krishna's own tribe, the Yâdavas, chiefly as regards marriage, are notorious.[4]

It is thus possible that they may have largely absorbed some of the Dravidian or indigenous races among whom, as we have seen, black stone worship was prevalent. In fact there seems reason to believe that this element in the

[1] Pliny, *Nat. Hist.*, ii., 59; *Asiatic Researches*, iv., 388; Burton, *Pilgrimage*, ii., 300 *seqq.*; Shea-Troyer, *Dabistan*, i., 49; Burckhardt, *Travels*, i., 172, 249 *seqq.*; Crooke, *loc. cit.*, i., 82; *Panjab Notes and Queries*, ii., 145.

[2] Schuyler, *Turkistan*, ii., 113; i., 138.

[3] Frazer, *Literary History of India*, 216 *note*; *Mahâbhârata*, *Kavna Parva*, lxxxiii., 17; Ray, trans., vi., 316.

[4] Ragendralâla Mitra, *Indo Aryans*, i., 425.

Krishna cult is more prominent than is generally suspected. The Madura of Southern India is supposed to take its name from the Dravidian Madur, "Old town," and the Krishna cult to have been derived from that of the Southern Indian Kurappan, "the black one."[1] If this be so, the more famous Mathura of the North would be an offshoot from the southern shrine, a development the reverse of popular belief. And the Sanskrit derivation of the former, "the place of milking," may have been a later invention when a cult of kine was added to the ruder form of worship. It is noticeable that the connection between the teachers of Mathura and the Madras Brâhmans is even now well marked.

At any rate, whatever may be the genesis of the dark-hued Krishna, it is clear that his legends absorbed much of the popular folk-beliefs which in this paper I have tried to illustrate.

WEDNESDAY, NOVEMBER 15th, 1899.

Mr. G. L. GOMME, Vice-President, in the Chair.

THE minutes of the last Meeting of the Society, and of the Joint Meeting of the Anthropological Institute and the Society held on the 27th June, were read and confirmed.

The election of Mr. E. Vincent Evans, Miss C. Burdon, and Mr. A. Shewan as members of the Society was announced.

The resignation of Professor C. de la Saussaye was also announced.

The Secretary exhibited on behalf of the President a photograph of Professor Starr and his two boys, Manuel and Louis.

[1] Senâthi Râja, *Journal of the Royal Asiatic Society*, xix, 578, *note* 3; Frazer, *Literary History*, 304 *note*.

Dr. Gaster exhibited 150 chap-books and some broadsides and folk-songs he had collected during a recent visit to Italy, and related some of his experiences while collecting them.

The Secretary read a note by Mr. C. G. Seligmann on a Bull-Roarer in Ceylon.

Mr. R. R. Marett then read a paper entitled, "Preanimistic Religion;" and a discussion followed, in which Mr. Clodd, Mr. Nutt, Dr. Gaster, and the Chairman took part.

A vote of thanks was accorded to Mr. Marett for his paper.

WEDNESDAY, DECEMBER 20th, 1899.

Mr. G. L. GOMME, Vice-President, in the Chair.

THE minutes of the last Meeting were read and confirmed.

The election of Mr. T. Thorp, Mr. A. W. Ebbs, Mrs. C. Bond, and Miss K. Higford, as members of the Society was announced.

The deaths of Dr. Brinton and the Rev. E. Owen, and the resignations of Mr. W. J. Knowles, Mr. E. H. Man, and Mr. J. A. Strong, were also announced.

Mr. C. A. Myers exhibited a number of lantern-slides illustrating the scenery and some types and customs of the residents of Murray Island, Torres Straits; and subsequently read a paper entitled "An Account of Two Obsolete Ceremonies in the Medicine and Sorcery of Murray Island." In the discussion which followed, Mr. Nutt, Mr. Higgens, Miss Burne, and the Chairman took part. The Meeting concluded with a vote of thanks to Mr. Myers for his paper.

The following books were reported as having been presented to the Society since the June Meeting, viz.:

L'Ile d'Amorgos, by H. Hauttecœur; *A Study of the Census of the Pueblo of Cochiti*, *The Little Pottery Objects of Lake Chapala*, *Notched Bones from Mexico*, *The Mapa de Cuanhtlantzinco or Códice Campos*, *Aztec Place Names*, *The Aztecs of Ancient Mexico*, and *Some North American Spear-Throwers*, all by Professor Starr, presented by the Author; *South Slavonic Folklore Stories*, and *North-West Slav Legends and Fairy Tales*, both by W. W. Strickland, presented by the Author; the *Bulletin de la Société Neuchateloise de Geographie*, tom. ix., presented by the Society; vol. v., parts 3 and 4, of *Lud: Organ Towarzystwa Ludoznawezego we Lwowie*; *A Country Schoolmaster*, *J. Shaw*, by Professor Wallace, presented by the Author; *Byegones relating to Wales and the Border Counties*, 1897, 1898, presented by the Editor; *Deutsches Krankheitsnamen-Buch*, by Dr. M. Höfler, presented by the Author; *Actes de la Société Philologique*, vol. xxiii., *Le Folklore dans les deux Mondes*, by the Comte de Charencey, presented by the Society; *Annual Report of British New Guinea*, 1894-1897 (4 volumes), presented by the Agent-General for Queensland; the *Administration Report for the Madras Government Museum*, 1898, 1899, presented by the Madras Government; *Bojagic Aldles Glück und Grab*, and *Haarschurgodschaft bei den Süd- slaven*, both by Dr. F. S. Krauss, presented by the President; *The Secular and Ceremonial Dances of Torres Straits*, by Professor Haddon, also presented by the President; *I Zpráva o cinnosti Národopisného Musea Ceskoslovanského*, by Dr. Lubor Niederle; *Prispevky K. Dejinam Narodopisu Ceskoslovanského*, by Fr. ad Subert; *Transactions of the Japan Society*, vol. iii., presented by the Society; *Archivio della R. Società Romana di Storia Patria*, vol. xx., parts 1 and 2, presented by the Society; *Guide to Queensland*, presented by the Agent-General for Queensland; *Report of the Seventh Meeting of the Australasian Association for the Advancement of Science*, presented by the Association; *International Catalogue of Scientific Literature* (*Queensland*), by J. Shirley, presented by the Agent-General for Queensland; and *Dansk Bondeliv*, by the Rev. H. F. Feilberg, presented by the Author.

WEDNESDAY, JANUARY 17th, 1900.

THE 22nd ANNUAL MEETING, which was also a SPECIAL GENERAL MEETING of the Society.

THE PRESIDENT (Mr. E. S. Hartland) in the Chair.

THE minutes of the last Annual Meeting were read and confirmed.

The Annual Report, Statement of Accounts, and Balance Sheet for the year 1899 were duly presented, and upon the motion of Mr. Nutt, seconded by Mr. Emslie, it was resolved that the same be received and adopted.

Balloting papers for the election of President, Vice-Presidents, Council, and Officers for the year 1900 having been distributed, Mr. Kirby and the Secretary were, on the motion of Mr. Nutt, seconded by Mr. Emslie, appointed scrutineers for the ballot.

Upon the motion of the President, seconded by Mr. Gomme, it was unanimously resolved that the following new rules be adopted and added to the rules of the Society, viz. :—

(A) The property of the Society shall be vested in three trustees.

(B) The first trustees shall be appointed at a Meeting convened for the purpose.

(C) The office of trustee shall be vacated (i) by resignation in writing addressed to the Secretary, and (ii) by removal at a Meeting of Members convened for the purpose.

(D) The Meeting removing a trustee shall appoint another in his place. Vacancies in the office arising by death or resignation shall be filled up by the Council.

(E) No trustee shall be responsible for any loss arising to the Society from any cause other than his own wilful act or default.

Upon the motion of Mr. Gomme, seconded by Mr. Kirby, it was resolved that Mr. Edward Clodd, Mr. Edward William

Brabrook, C.B., and Mr. James E. Crombie be appointed the first trustees of the Society, pursuant to Rule (B).

The President delivered his Presidential Address, the subject being "Totemism and some Recent Discoveries."

A hearty vote of thanks having been accorded to the President for his address, upon the motion of Mr. Clodd, seconded by Mr. Gomme, the result of the ballot was announced by the Secretary, and the following ladies and gentlemen who had been nominated by the Council were declared to have been elected, viz.:

As *President:* Mr. E. S. Hartland.

As *Vice-Presidents:* The Hon. J. Abercromby, the Rt. Hon. Lord Avebury, Miss C. S. Burne, Mr. Clodd, Mr. G. Laurence Gomme, Mr. A. Nutt, Lieut.-Gen. Pitt-Rivers, Professor F. York Powell, Professor J. Rhys, the Rev. Professor A. H. Sayce, and Professor E. B. Tylor.

As *Members of Council:* Mr. H. Courthope Bowen, Miss Lucy Broadwood, Mr. E. K. Chambers, Mr. F. C. Conybeare, Mr. J. E. Crombie, Mr. W. Crooke, Mr. F. T. Elworthy, Dr. Gaster, Mr. T. Gowland, Miss F. Grove, Professor Haddon, Mr. T. W. E. Higgens, Miss E. Hull, Professor F. B. Jevons, Professor W. P. Ker, Mr. A. F. Major, Mr. S. E. Bouverie-Pusey, Mr. W. H. D. Rouse, Professor B. C. A. Windle, and Mr. A. R. Wright.

As *Hon. Treasurer:* Mr. E. W. Brabrook.

As *Hon. Auditor:* Mr. F. G. Green.

As *Secretary:* Mr. F. A. Milne.

Upon the motion of Professor York Powell, seconded by Mr. Wright, it was resolved that a hearty vote of thanks be accorded to the retiring Members of the Council, viz. Mr. C. J. Billson, Dr. Karl Blind, Mr. Leland L. Duncan, Mr. Emslie, Mr. Jacobs, Mr. Ordish, and Mr. Wheatley.

The President laid on the table the *Ethnographical Album of the Native Races of Southern Mexico*, presented to the Society by Professor Starr, and referred to in the Presidential Address.